Praise for *Climate Grief*

"'As climate science continued to prove true, how would we cope as individuals and as a society?' Thankfully Weaver dedicated her life to answering questions like this one so that we could each benefit from the wisdom in her findings. More than an exploration of climate change and its impact on our mental health, this book eloquently and practically outlines how to thrive despite the seemingly insurmountable odds. If one's psyche is enmeshed with one's surroundings, as Weaver states, then surely, we all owe it to each other to surround ourselves with this book, which at once educates, inspires, unites, and comforts. A must-read for anyone who craves a healthier future for all."

—**Julie Schnedeker**, author, Cofounder of Plant-Based Point

"Weaver's pertinent observations that our inner life is inextricably woven into the life of the physical world of nature is ever more important in this day of reckless damage to most of the Earth's ecosystems. She thoughtfully provides clues and answers to a world in which nature's health is indeed a taproot of our own mental health."

—**Terril L. Shorb**, Ph.D., author, Faculty Emeritus at Prescott College

"There is no shortage of books that outline the depressing pace of climate change on our planet. This beautifully written, hopeful book breaks new ground. Acknowledging the science of our declining ecosystems, and the grief that comes with it, Shawna writes in equal parts as a scientist, activist, ecotherapist, and poet. It's as if Greta Thunberg, Annie Dillard, Elizabeth Kubler Ross, and Rachel Carson were rolled into one. Using both Midwestern practicality and dynamic vision, this book takes us on a personal journey using ecotherapy and reconnection to the natural world to overcome our collective climate grief. In the process we find healing for ourselves, our communities, and our planet. If you read only one book this year, please let it be this one."

—**Seth Tibbott**, author, Founder of Tofurkey

CLIMATE GRIEF

From Coping to
Resilience and Action

Shawna Weaver, PhD

Lantern Publishing & Media ● Woodstock and Brooklyn, NY

2023
Lantern Publishing & Media
PO Box 1350
Woodstock, NY 12498
www.lanternpm.org

Cover design by Melissa Weisser

Printed in the United States of America

Library of Congress Cataloging-in-Publication Data

Names: Weaver, Shawna, author.
Title: Climate grief : from coping to resilience and action / Shawna Weaver.
Description: Woodstock, NY : Lantern Publishing & Media, 2023. |
    Includes bibliographical references.
Identifiers: LCCN 2023001794 (print) | LCCN 2023001795 (ebook) |
    ISBN 9781590567166 (paperback) | ISBN 9781590567173 (epub)
Subjects: LCSH: Climatic changes—Social aspects. | Climatic changes—
    Prevention—Citizen participation. | Global environmental change—
    Psychological aspects. | Environmental psychology. | Climatic
    changes—Psychological aspects.
Classification: LCC BF353.5.C55 W43 2023 (print) | LCC BF353.5.C55
    (ebook) | DDC 155.9/15—dc23/eng/20230124
LC record available at https://lccn.loc.gov/2023001794
LC ebook record available at https://lccn.loc.gov/2023001795

TABLE OF CONTENTS

About the Author
About the Publisher

FOREWORD

Mary Bue

Musician, Climate-Change Activist

In a moment of despair in the midst of my teenage wasteland, I walked into the deep forest on my parents' land in central Minnesota. Kept mostly as a preserve, the tall pines stand silent, except never really silent as the wind that blows through their needles makes the most glorious music. I had survived a car wreck the week before, rolling my car into a deep ditch and hanging upside down from my seat belt, windshield and windows smashed, somehow safely cocooned in the Buick LeSabre, emerging without a scratch from the wreckage.

After this car wreck, I felt tremendous survivor guilt. Though no one had been hurt, not even my physical body, I wondered why it was that I happened to survive while so many die from similar accidents. My sixteen-year-old heart fell into a depression that I didn't fully understand.

In my suicidal ideation, my search for meaning in the forest, I saw the fiery orange of the monarch butterfly alight on the white pines. So many of them. The branches were lit up, flickering and fluttering like candles. A kaleidoscope. A miracle.

The hope that this vision brought me was paramount. Angel butterflies, reminding me that there is so much beauty and wonder to behold in this life on earth. I titled my first album *Where the Monarchs Circled* (2000) after this special place with multiple tattoos to follow, ever as reminders, that the beauty of nature can bring solace, connection, and the will to continue forth upon this crazy challenging life.

How many of us have wandered lost into the forest and emerged with newfound hope? No doubt people have searched for a sign by the millions, like the butterflies once migrated by the millions.

Each autumn in the western hemisphere, the migratory monarch butterfly (Danaus plexippus), a subspecies of the monarch butterfly, take an awe-inspiring journey of 4,000-5,000 kilometers from southern Canada to the forests of Mexico to winter. There are multiple migratory routes, and one of them happens to be down the central corridor of the United States through Minnesota, where I currently live and where I witnessed that kaleidoscopic miracle. A nonprofit called Monarch Joint Venture, working to protect the monarch migration across the United States, has denoted Interstate 35 as "The Monarch Highway"—a symbolic migration corridor that follows Interstate 35 (I-35) from Laredo, Texas, to Duluth, Minnesota (where Shawna and I met), aligning with the central flyway of the eastern migratory population of the monarch butterfly.

I say that these incredible insects once migrated by the millions because as of 2022, they have been added to the International Union for Conservation of Nature (IUCN) Red List of Threatened Species™ as Endangered, threatened by habitat destruction and climate change. The western population is at greatest risk of extinction, having declined by an estimated 99.9 percent, from as many as 10 million to 1,914 butterflies between the 1980s and 2021. The larger eastern population also shrunk by 84 percent from 1996 to 2014. Concern remains as to whether enough butterflies survive to maintain the populations and prevent extinction.

The forests in Mexico where they winter as well as their summer breeding grounds in United States and Canada are threatened by deforestation by both legal and illegal logging for agriculture and urban development. Herbicides and pesticides in intensive farming along their migratory corridors kill the butterflies themselves as well as their diet of milkweed, the host plant that the larvae of the monarch butterfly feed on, as well as other nectar-producing pollinator-friendly plants. Extreme weather events linked to climate change such as droughts, catastrophic fires, extreme temperatures which trigger premature migrations before food is available for them, and severe storms which are increasing as our temperatures rise, also play a role in their reduction.

Endangered species have always hurt my heart. I just want to wrap all of the beautiful furry, feathery, scaly, sharp, tusked creatures in my arms and carry them across to safety. But, to where? Don't tell me now that it's too late.

I met Dr. Shawna Weaver just over a decade ago in Duluth, Minnesota. We were both vegans, which is a quite small community in Duluth, and bonded immediately with our love of music, study, travel, writing, and food. We run together, journey abroad together, dine, cook, laugh, cry, and talk of everything under the sun. The connection between veganism and sustainability has been a deep bond for us and the knowledge that eating plant-based foods, is not only better for our heart, but also has a lower environmental impact than consuming animal products.

According to Harvard TH ChanSchool of Public Health (2022), "Participants who consumed healthy plant-based diets had lower cardiovascular disease risk, and those diets had lower greenhouse gas emissions and use of cropland, irrigation water, and nitrogenous fertilizer than diets that were higher in unhealthy plant-based and animal-based foods." This is one of the many ways Shawna presents as coming to grips and action in facing our time-sensitive dilemma.

We are intrinsically linked to nature. Let your consciousness rotate around these images, like a poem. Walking through a forest, with crisp air and a butterfly migration. Traversing a Nebraska highway devastatingly packed with cattle, stinking sky high with excrement . . . notice the feelings that arise. A vast desert, a vibrant metro sky high with buildings. Calm blue sky or swirling dangerous tornadoes. The winter that doesn't end. The summer that breaks your AC, nowhere to turn in the thick heat, your neighbors dropping like flies in high-rises. Gridlock. Jackhammers pounding. Painstakingly wiping oil off seabirds after a spill. Once pristine beaches now rainbow pebbles of plastic bits. An old shoe washed up on a beach. Islands of plastic.

A moment in time that gave me so much hope, a place in nature that I return to again and again in my mind, has drastically changed with that reality check. The butterflies. Are endangered. Because of us. Nature, of which we are an integral part, which feeds us, clothes us, provides us shelter, our home, our environment . . . it is changing, and changing fast. And it is so, SO hard to handle.

What Shawna provides us with in *Climate Grief: From Coping to Resilience and Action* is a template with which to understand the sorrow of the degradation of much of our beautiful planetary home. To accept, and to ultimately find meaning and inspire change.

I often think of the struggle of the butterfly emerging from the chrysalis during its eclosion. It cannot be helped by outside forces. The act of the struggle is what hardens the wings and allows it to fly. So, while we separately come to our own conclusions, we push through and onward and outward in the struggle, we have many choices, and also, as in the framework of grief, many stages to work through. I found once on the side of the road a hand-scribbled note that said, "The struggle is part of the story." The most important thing is the meaning. And also, the connection. The collective migration down the corridor of the heart, toward meaning. There may be just a few of us left at the moment, as it may feel that way at times. Our numbers may be dwindling. However, there are many of us who still care, and still hope. Acceptance is key as we sort out our way. The planet holds wisdom and power greater than any of us, and is showing us, always, who's boss. Can we live in concert with the beauty, majesty, awe, and bliss mingling amongst the terror, heartbreak, uncertainty, and change?

Allow Dr. Shawna Weaver's wisdom, compassion, heartfelt truth, scholarship, experience, and activism be a trusted guide as we navigate the waters of our great planet's—and our own—evolution. Like a bridge over troubled water, as Shawna writes, "just taking the next best step," linking our truth and actions with our heart can bring hope and healing. Yes, the future of our species is uncertain. Yes, the beautiful places and beings as we know them dwindle. So tempting to fall to nihilism, to Dionysus-style excess in "apocalypse mentality". . . and yet, those of us with wings to fly can still make a kaleidoscope of comfort, support, beauty, and hope. For the love of Mother Earth, honoring the one in the many, each voice in this struggle is valid and each stage in the process is real. I hope that in this book you feel seen, heard and understood, and know that the depth of your grief is equal to the depth of your love.

Preface

I grew up in the 1980s in the headwaters region of Lake Superior, the North Woods of the Upper Midwest, with its countless small lakes, rivers, and bogs, which shaped who I am and how I see the world. I remember, as a kid, snowmobiling through national forests, camping next to pristine creeks, and looking for agates and toads along the shorelines during the summer; there were so many toads hopping across the roads at night that I'd beg my dad to swerve around them. I remember hearing loons in the evening, calling to each other across the calm waters with a haunting elegance. Later in the night, owls and coyotes, usually softer and further in the distance, would take the stage, accompanied by a chorus of crickets and small wetland creatures.

My parents introduced me to the local ecosystem through our quiet adventures in the woods and gave me hours of free time to explore. It was easy to appreciate nature in the Upper Midwest, where many parts of the ecosystem appeared to be thriving. Given the huge swaths of lush green forests, abundance of streams, and highly dynamic seasonal weather here, it was hard to imagine a lack of water or food. Even harder for me to imagine was feeling separated from nature, because an extreme climate like this one demanded constant physical attention. The summer was humid and daylight stretched well past bedtime, playing my circadian rhythm to the polarity of the northern solstice. The autumn was illuminated by golden birch, sepia oak, and enough tamarack and

maple to splash every possible hue of arboreal color across the
horizon. With a backdrop of evergreen cedars and pines, the Upper
Midwest gave a grand albeit short fall finale as it surrendered to
an endlessly white, frigid, unrelenting winter. Winter winds would
creep through drifting snow and cut into my breath, seeping into
my eyes, nose, lungs, and bones, finding their way through every
seam in every layer. Back then, snow piles persisted in the corners
of shady hillsides and parking lots well into the month of June.
Now, snowy winters are less common, and extreme temperatures
accompany a years-long warming trend.

As an industrial region, Northeast Minnesota has scars of the
timber industry scratched across it, leaving fields of pine stumps
around patches of old growth, remnants of an ecosystem that once
stood much taller. Railroad tracks crisscross small towns leading
to the ports, and shipping is active for several months of the year.
Shiploads of taconite pellets from mining are dumped onto loading
docks, and, until an explosion temporarily halted operations, an
oil refinery constantly burned off methane about a few miles from
my childhood home. I remember that the summer after third
grade, a train carrying petroleum by-products derailed over a
river, causing a benzine oil spill and forcing evacuations. The day
became known as "Toxic Tuesday," as the benzine cloud made
the town's air unbreathable. While the companies involved have
always been quiet about the incident, the resulting environmental
degradation and cases of cancer in humans continue today.

At the time of the spill, my family was out of town, at our
cabin just ninety miles away, looking for agates and toads while
enjoying the sounds of summer evenings. While our neighbors
at home were clamoring to avoid acute catastrophe following
the benzine spill, the subtle signs of climate change had already
taken hold of the region. The older generation lamented the slow

disappearance of frogs, the increase in disease-carrying ticks, and the clear-cut lots making way for more and more development. So many small signals would force us to notice that we were headed for significant changes. As I started fourth grade, there was a surge of interest in environmental protection. Our school music concert was focused on the environment, and we learned a song that, while I do not remember its name or any other lyrics, had two lines that still occasionally find their way into my mind in quiet moments of my adult life, thousands of miles away from my hometown:

Oil and water, they just don't mix, that's a guarantee;
Fish and wildlife get very sick from sea to shining sea.

I remember that school year was the first time I heard a national news story about climate change. I remember riding in the car with my mom and crossing the bridge that connects Wisconsin and Minnesota over the St. Louis River Bay, the Great Lakes' primary water supply. A *Public Radio* show was covering news about a hole in the ozone layer. Peering out the window at the vast sky stretching out above the water, each reflecting the light blues and grays in the other, I wondered what a hole in the sky would look like. I imagined a looming black hole that could suck up all the water, all the trees, and all the colors. It was a terrifying moment of imagination and clarity—a realization that the world as I knew it was not so idyllic, and, worse yet, the people in charge of it were far from infallible. I would soon begin to understand that these leaders weren't just fallible but were nefarious in their lack of concern for our climate.

From there, I started to notice changes. I noticed fewer frogs on the road. I observed later fall colors and stronger storms. I detected news headlines starting to feature more disturbing estimates, such as the prediction that by 2050 there would be more plastic than life in the oceans. I watched small farms in Minnesota get replaced by massive factory farms. I heard about the Keeling Curve, the monitoring system alerting us to escalating levels of CO_2 in the atmosphere. I heard about climate refugees as rising seas absorbed faraway islands.

Climate grief grew like a silent drumbeat deep in my interior world. The habitat loss and deforestation, animal cruelty, pollution, and extreme weather in my own community that I witnessed haunted me throughout my childhood. More compelling to me than the science itself was how humans reacted to such information. The plight of planet Earth seemed so clear to me that I could not ignore it, but that wasn't true for others. As climate science grew more convincing, divisions in society became more apparent. I found it fascinating that there were earnest attempts to argue against factual information—facts that seemed to simply confirm what was already so intuitive and obvious. I questioned: Was the truth so painful that people actively chose to deny it to protect their own sense of safety? Was the science too difficult to understand? Did people need to experience and love nature for themselves in order to help science come to life? Were there more sinister motivations behind denial? As climate science continued to prove true, how would we cope as individuals and as a society?

By the time I entered college, I knew these were the questions I wanted to spend my career working to answer. My path forward was as unclear as the questions themselves were difficult. Was I meant to be a scientist? A sociologist, a researcher, or a therapist of some sort? As I sought a career path, I also considered these questions for my own sake as I coped with my worries about the planet. I explored spirituality and psychology for coping mechanisms to dampen my frustration with how people were reacting to climate change and to calm my own reaction. I also dug into climate science. While the news and research were overwhelming, building my understanding of the facts helped me emotionally. What I was going through was *climate grief*: a sense that as climate changed, so too would my experience of the world. This is what climate change does to all of us. The world as we know it is changing for the worse, which we cannot control, and loss will be inevitable. I felt all of that then, along with the increasing urgency to do something. I realized I wanted to study people and nature—people *in* nature—but that still felt too impractical, too unconventional. I spent my undergraduate years trying to find an academic place to put this curiosity, which led to enough credits for multiple minors and majors; yet none quite fit.

By my senior year, I was finding myself in a labyrinth of knowledge spread thinly across multiple fields in which I did not belong, and lacking a clear career path. The human–nature connection was what I wanted to think about, yet it was a subject with no undergraduate home. From there, I found my way to graduate school. The goal was to earn my degree in mental health counseling so that I could help people better show up for the planet and for themselves. I was not satisfied with the premise that good mental health boiled down to behavioral change, brain functioning, and medication. I knew that one's surroundings, including the natural world, played a significant part in determining mental health. I also believed that depression and anxiety that surfaced in response to experience were not the problems to solve. Surely, I wasn't alone in this belief. Surely, one's psyche must be enmeshed with one's surroundings. If an unhealthy family life contributes to creating mental health issues, what of an unhealthy natural environment? I had heard of graduate programs that wove together ecological justice, psychospirituality, wilderness therapies, and even fields like transpersonal psychology. I wished, against my Midwestern practicality, to pursue such audacious studies. These programs seemed to me to be reaching for something deeper, something I was trying to find. Yet, I did not have the boldness to assume that I belonged in such a fascinating and cutting-edge program, or that I could make a difference doing something so unconventional and unheard of. There was something in these programs that piqued my soul, even as a sense of guilt and fear of the untraditional held me to something more immediately tangible and resonant with my upbringing.

The building I entered on my first day of graduate school was an underwhelming, retrofitted office building. It was so utilitarian and uninspiring, it could have been mistaken for a clinic or an accounting firm, not at all conducive to the romantic excitement of my graduate school hopes. In previous years, when I had dared to dream about graduate school, I had never imagined myself in such an unassuming setting. Alas, here I was, making a practical, uninspiring decision to be in a *traditional* psychology program. (More on following your truth and making wholehearted decisions later in this book.) As I sat in the old office-building classroom, waiting for my first Theories of Personality class to start, I at least felt that psychology was the right path for me. Plus, studying such a drab ecosystem as the one I was in ought to bring insight into how humans respond to their environment! Yes, without a doubt, I would find a way to explore human psychology around *nature*, and surely, I would find others doing the same.

Class started, and the professor instructed us to share our names and what specifically we intended to study. The room was filled with people who were already in some sort of social-work field and looking for advancement, and with folks who wanted to start a private counseling practice. My turn came and I said, "I want to incorporate nature into psychological healing and to explore how healing people can heal nature." While I knew that my poetic idea lacked specificity, I wanted to ground myself in something theoretical. Unlike in a traditional psychology track, which equips students to be able to diagnose illnesses and prescribe medication or conduct talk therapy, I was hoping to explore and solve the specific problem of the human–nature relationship. I was convinced there was room in mainstream psychology for me. The professor, however, cocked his gaze upward and said: "I'm not sure that is something you will find. Good luck." He shrugged and moved on to the person next to me while my face burned with embarrassment.

While I would eventually find my niche, it would be another handful of years as a counselor, an academic, and then an activist before I made my way to ecopsychology. As it turned out, since about the 1960s, psychologists had been establishing a theoretical framework that merges psychology and ecology to promote sustainability. Until I found these people and the impressive body of their wisdom, I had woven into my counseling work every nature-adjacent tool I could find. I had convinced organizations I worked for to build outdoor classrooms, or I had created my own. I had trained therapy dogs. I had filled my office with plants. I had taken note of the many times my clients would lament about daily life in an urbanized, mechanized world, expressing their desire to be in the woods, to swim, to get their hands dirty. Finally, I found Prescott College, where I would earn a Ph.D. in sustainability education. Prescott offered the unapologetically progressive, tradition-bucking, innovative program I had dreamed of before. Bad traditions have led us into the messes we find ourselves in. As I learned very early on, to build a lifestyle that sustains us, we must stop upholding an expectation of ourselves that we don't even like. I hadn't done myself any favors in pursuing a program that seemed practical but didn't fit my core values or goals.

Empowered by my experience at Prescott, I started an ecotherapy center, complete with therapy chickens, gardens, and a yard full of sustainability experiments. Here, clients would learn permaculture approaches to gardening, and we would co-create a corner of the world where everything in the system had its purpose and where nothing went to waste. We would wander the woods together and sit next to the streams, and clients would be allowed to sort through their struggles. I met a few other ecotherapists, scattered around the world, and found a level of hope I had never felt. I found a community of like-minded people who also questioned our modern lifestyle, mourned our disconnect from nature, and feared the consequences of a changing climate.

I discovered the grief I felt about climate change was not unique. In fact, I met professionals who were pushing for the American Psychological Association to establish climate grief as a diagnosis. It has been a messy journey—for me career-wise and for most others involved—but one that has really finally just begun. While climate grief may be finding its way into headlines, we are nowhere near prepared for coping with climate change or the grief born from it. The field of psychology is not prepared and our society is not prepared. We aren't prepared for the changes themselves, let alone for their emotional and mental repercussions.

Years after proudly belting out the words "oil and water, they just don't mix" with only a vague understanding of what they meant, I started writing this book. I wrote it because throughout my twenties, I yearned to find an academic place to ask questions about how we humans can reconnect with nature, to find perspectives on how we can live our lives sustainably. I realize these questions are spiritual and existential as much as they are emotional and intellectual. In my education, research, and work spanning counseling and ecotherapy, I have met countless people doing amazing things for the planet. But for each of them, I have met many more people who do not understand how to cope with climate grief or how to mitigate climate change.

I have spent plenty of time standing on the sidelines, confused about how to get involved, while struggling to find my niche and feeling powerless and isolated. I still often feel that way. Those of us already mired in the sadness and anxiety of climate grief, already consumed, occasionally or even frequently, by dread, may feel stuck in a system of human greed and ignorance, guided by an insistence on prioritizing capital and growth over sustainability. The realities of our society are not conducive to our making decisions with hopeful hearts. Despite the helplessness we feel at times, having a community of like-hearted humans lends itself to optimism.

I am convinced that all of us experience climate grief. By embracing the truth of our situation and the hard emotions it gives rise to, we find untapped motivation and skills that enable us to help our planet. As we mourn together and strategize together, we may also be reawakened to holistic wellness within ourselves and with nature. If, indeed, we are suffering an unacknowledged detachment from our source, we must first look to the natural world around us. Whether or not we can save what remains, it is not too late to learn what might be possible if we try. And if we *do* reconnect with nature in time to save life on Earth as we know it, imagine how much future generations will benefit from our efforts today. Whatever our next step, unprocessed climate grief may be the greatest barrier keeping us from a better, healthier future together. Healing the planet starts with healing ourselves.

INTRODUCTION

Climate grief is not a pathology but a reasonable, rational response to living in an increasingly unstable environment. Scientists refer to the current era as the Anthropocene, characterized by the dominant influence of human activity on the environment and climate. To live in the Anthropocene is to experience rapid change, intense competition, and significant loss. Climate grief is the emotional experience of losing a predictable, sustainable climate. It can be triggered by extreme events, such as hurricanes, droughts, and wildfires, or by the ambiguity of subtle changes and an unknown future.

Climate grief can be experienced by climate scientists, activists, kids—anybody who understands or fears the negative effects of climate change. Many around the world are losing their livelihood, even their entire community, to unprecedented natural disasters, directly experiencing grief as significant causal effects of climate change literally hit home. Some of us are luckier. But although our position on the planet right now may afford us the privilege of reliable food and water sources and of safety, nothing is a guarantee. Mother Nature can change our reality without notice, especially given our quickly changing geopolitical environment. Just worrying about how bad things could be in the future can lead one to feel powerless, fearful, exhausted, even burned out.

As acknowledgment of climate change grows, climate grief is also a growing phenomenon, which is only logical: these new realities inevitably come with an emotional toll when we pay even just a little attention. If we, as a society, are to deal with climate change, we must acknowledge climate grief. Successfully mitigating climate grief and climate change requires working through them simultaneously. It is how we cope with and move through grief that determines whether we can integrate that grief into a lifestyle that contributes to solving the problem of climate change.

While we focus on this work individually, we can support each other in grieving and ending unsustainable practices within our control, and we can also strengthen our pressure on bigger players. Governments and corporations should be held responsible for halting larger-scale climate-disrupting practices, as well as for supporting communities' healing. No change happens without our strength in numbers, or without commitment and resolve. In my time working with climate activists, scientists, and therapists, a clear pattern of coping strategies emerged. This book is meant to help you, the reader, explore your climate grief and find such strategies to mitigate it as we work to also mitigate climate change.

The first strategy, or task, is to learn more about climate change. Understand the science that tells us the big picture, and understand the details in your local ecosystem. To heal anxiety, we must uncover gaps in our knowledge so we can focus our worries on reality rather than the much broader scope of unknowns. Doing yourself the favor of separating real risks from fears will go a long way in anxiety management. If you're already well-versed in climate science (hence your anxieties), focus on news about promising inventions, inspiring innovations, and local success stories. These realities are underrepresented in our fear-based news culture.

Next, take the time to understand your grief. Uncomfortable as it may be for us to process our emotions, grief informs us about the problem and propels our creative thinking toward solutions. The "why" behind a problem—what makes it a problem—can be found in our bodies' reaction to it. Problems often get needlessly complex because we don't have or use the needed tools—such as empathy, healthy communication, and self-regulation—to solve them while they're simpler. In spite of our growing understanding of mental health issues, emotional healthcare is not valued enough in modern industrialized cultures, and grief is largely ignored. Thus, embracing and exploring the depths of our emotional experiences will be a critical part of the healing work we do individually and as a community.

The third task in order to cope with grief is to create a well-being strategy. Once you identify your grief, coping is a constant, daily, forever practice. You practice coping with any loss or anxiety until it, or your body, passes away. Climate grief will require a daily practice of self-care, emotional growth, and anything that you discover serves your health. It takes effort to cope; anybody who has healed from trauma or loss has put in the work to do so. What does it mean to be healing, or to have healed? Healing is indicated by an increasingly relaxed physiological response to triggers and by an ability to follow through with healthy practices. Insight, together with intention and practice, is the path to healing.

Finally, ignite a passion and motivation to do active healing work for others and the environment. Realign yourself within your community as a climate change activist. This does not mean you have to quit your job and chain yourself to trees for months on end, though for some of us, it might. For the rest of us, it might mean focusing on mental health and relationship building in our current lives and communities. Our next steps may include slowing down in daily life and re-evaluating what is truly important, so that we can reduce the capitalist pressure to keep contributing to unsustainable growth. Coping with climate grief requires not just focusing inward but also putting in serious effort to curb climate change across all sectors and in all countries. We can't—we must not—let our physical and emotional landscapes keep deteriorating. As more and more of us shift our perspectives toward hope and action, we will see our hard work pay off in the form of an upward cultural spiral. The more we heal ourselves and our communities—microcosms of the world—the more we heal our planet.

Chapters 1 through 4 of this book—"The Coming of Global Climate Change," "Getting to Know Climate Grief," "Tools for Resilience and Well-Being," and "Where Do We Go from Here?"—will dive into each of the above four tasks.

I

THE COMING OF GLOBAL CLIMATE CHANGE

"We are making choices that will affect whether beings
thousands of generations from now will be able to be born
sound of mind and body."—**Joanna Macy** (environmental
activist, scholar, pioneer of deep ecology)

Drastic, human-caused environmental destabilization has altered
life as we know it and will increasingly affect us directly. As a
result, we humans are experiencing emotional consequences as
we simultaneously cause and mourn these changes in climate.
Weather patterns, air and water safety, food availability, and
biodiversity have all changed in recent decades: this is the new
normal.

Climate change and climate grief are among the most
profound problems for our species today. I can't imagine a
scenario in which we wouldn't be dealing with climate change
and its emotional impact well into the lifetimes of future
generations. Previous mass extinctions occurred long before our
time; in all of human history, rarely have communities of humans
experienced a total and inescapable ecosystem collapse, such that
we now face.[1] We have wreaked so much havoc on the planet so

quickly that it has been proposed that we establish a new epoch in geological history, called the Anthropocene, to separate it from the preceding Holocene.

The Holocene encompasses the 11,700 years since the end of the last ice age. The retreat of glaciers allowed for more human movement and migration, leading to population growth, urbanization, the agricultural revolution, and the development of industry. Momentous as this global shift was, it pales in comparison to the mark we left in the planet's geology with the detonation of atomic bombs, which changed the chemical makeup of steel and other metals, changes that remain detectible in soils around the globe. Although there are varying takes on exactly when the Anthropocene began, it is undeniable that our influence on the planet during this new epoch has been more bad than good.

It has been a long time since I last spoke with someone who didn't have a strong opinion about climate change. As the scientific community continues to voice overwhelming agreement that the current environmental destabilization is human-caused, despite denial from the public and politicians, climate change has fought its way into our vernacular, having been an increasingly hot topic since the first Earth Day, a bipartisan effort, in 1970. After witnessing a devastating oil spill off the coast of Santa Barbara, junior senator Gaylord Nelson came up with the idea of college campus teach-ins about air and water pollution. He was a Democrat; his co-chair for the bill was a Republican. Their effort grew rapidly and, on April 22 of that year, unified countless groups across the country in what is now an annual, global initiative encompassing concentrated service projects and awareness campaigns. Since that first Earth Day, however, political energies around climate change have presented a frontline challenge in every sector, from business to religion. Climate change is all-encompassing, confusing, and overwhelming to grasp. It is, as Al Gore said, an inconvenient truth that we now have no choice but to face head-on.

Just as challenging as learning climate science is managing the emotional overwhelm caused by impending environmental collapse. Climate change is a household topic; its accompanying grief is not. Most people I spoke with while writing this book were not familiar with the term "climate grief." There was, though, a shared intuition about what it means. While we haven't yet fostered much discourse about climate grief, it is becoming a more and more obvious part of our daily lives, and the sense of shared grief I gathered from my conversations informed me just how badly we need this discussion. Increasingly, this collective grief is coming to the surface, whether or not there is a socially accepted framework for its presence. The sooner we make "climate grief" a household term, the easier it will be for us to work with it.

Reacting to Climate Change

Climate grief is the emotional toll of our reaction to climate change. We may refer to this range of emotions that we experience as *climate anxiety, pre-traumatic stress, apocalypse fatigue, ecological grief,* or by another name, but it is most often felt without being referred to at all. Up until this point, I have intentionally excluded a definition of climate grief. Sometimes, I think of climate grief as having leached into us, gradually sinking in—almost indistinguishable against other griefs in our internal landscape—and suddenly producing an inescapable influence on society. For many, this anxiety can be credited for changes in family planning, for relocations and migrations, career pivots, and general depression. While its symptoms are pervasive, transformative, and unlikely to retreat, the concept of climate grief is still emergent. It is not news to *everyone* though, as there are professionals who are dedicated to understanding the human connection with nature, who have been ahead of mainstream Western culture in anticipating both climate change and climate grief.

Ecopsychology is an interdisciplinary field established by practitioners who focus simultaneously on human health and planetary health.[2] Ecopsychologists and ecotherapists have long been responding to the emotional and physical repercussions of climate change. Ecopsychology covers a broad range of foci of study, including urban sustainability, human–animal interactions, the psychology of our connection to nature, and the psychology behind our environmental destruction. I hope we can look to ecopsychologists to lead the way in establishing more sustainable routes forward, perhaps starting with defining the multitude of climate-caused disorders—the anxiety, worry, post-traumatic stress following natural disasters, and general grief we experience, all of which are sparked by different aspects of climate change, and all of which carry their own sets of symptoms. Of all the ways in which we can describe our emotional responses to climate change, I focus on "grief" as a unifying term. My personal experience with climate change has included the waves of anger, sadness, bargaining, and acceptance common in the general grieving process. Climate change is a current reality, not a future possibility, so the anxiety we feel is our gut check. It's a call to action. Grief is the most appropriate description of this emotional state, as at the end of grief come a reintegration and a new perspective.

In my experience as a mental health practitioner, I've noticed a common theme among clients—dealing with grief.

In our culture, mental illness—with grief almost always playing a role—has long been a leading factor in physical illness, relational disconnection, and death. Among the worst harms we have done to ourselves is our dismissal of mental health as an afterthought, a luxury, a liability, or as nothing at all. Mental unwellness is enmeshed with all sorts of abuses, toxic behaviors in relationships, unhealthy cultural norms, and, yes, the way we mistreat our environment. As a sustainability specialist with a mental healthcare background, I now see that our harming ourselves plays a big role in climate change. Our disservice to the planet as the most destructive and disrespectful of its inhabitants in all of history reflects how we treat our own minds and bodies. The path to sustainability, to fixing our behaviors and cultural values, must be through mental healthcare.

Now, you may assume that mental healthcare is all about emotions, that only emotional people engage in mental healthcare. Some people tell me they don't like talking about feelings and they wouldn't know what to say in therapy. Mental healthcare is as much for those who describe themselves as left-brained or logical as it is for those who are more emotionally minded. Mental healthcare is more about intellectual processing, skill building, and problem solving than it is about reporting your feelings. It's about learning to control your thought patterns and integrate your emotions with your words and behaviors. Men, especially, have often told me of their journeys into mental healthcare—their hesitation to go to therapy due to heteronormative stereotypes and expectations, and their eventual appreciation for the process. Often, mental healthcare is about strategizing a path through the grieving process. Grief strikes us all, and regardless of your ability to express emotions outwardly, your mental health is a constant influence on your daily life.

Dealing with climate grief includes understanding what we are grieving (studying climate change), reducing what we have to grieve (working to lessen climate change), and working through the grief itself (learning to feel the feelings and cope with them). With any source of grief, be it a loved one's death, a medical prognosis, an ambiguous relationship, or now, climate change, knowing as many facts as possible helps us to grieve and cope. With knowledge, we make informed decisions and create a strategy.

Our emotional responses to climate change can hit hard because although our modern lifestyles suggest otherwise, humans and nature are inextricably connected. We exist on this planet with nearly nine million other species and trillions of individual beings at any given time, each of us the result of long evolutionary processes. We must admit that, viewed through any scientific or spiritual lens, the resilience of and the interconnection among all living beings are astonishing. Our existence relies on a specific and delicate balance of temperature and of oxygen, hydrogen, and carbon. As humans, we rarely regard ourselves as animals; however, we share the vast majority of our genetic makeup with other primates. We most easily obtain what we need nutritionally from plants—healthy plants, which require a healthy planet.[3] Weather impacts our moods, as sunny days energize us and cold weather tends to slow us down.[4] Seasons dictate our schedules, from the school year to meal times to social calendars.[5] Even the moon cycle affects our bodies and behaviors. Despite the many advances we've made, we still need bees to pollinate our crops;[6] we need the water to be free of deadly microbes and the topsoil to be nutrient-rich.[7,8] Humans are a needy species, with specific temperature and resource requirements and not much natural ability to survive in extreme conditions.

Human population growth is continuing undeterred as we tip the scales toward eight, nine billion people on the planet. We have added another billion people every twelve years over the past several decades, and the United Nations anticipates we will reach ten billion before the end of this century. Meanwhile, our resource needs have become increasingly taxing on the planet. Those of us in the wealthiest nations demand not just the basics, but comfort and even luxury. The global average of the amount of raw material used per person annually is more than ten metric tons, and the average carbon footprint is around sixteen tons in the United States. Consumerism's far-reaching influence means that more of us have distanced ourselves from subsistence living and from nature itself. At the same time, we are not good at realizing just how much we impact the planet, or at limiting ourselves when we've had enough or are demanding too much. Moderation is the very opposite of the self-indulgent values currently dictating our social norms.

The truth is: there are no shortcuts to learning the limits of our planet, managing our own behaviors, fortifying our own mental health, or fighting for better cultural norms. We have to commit to doing the learning (or unlearning) and doing the work. We need to manage our resource use by forming personal habits and socialized values that favor sustainability. Such realities as we now face aren't comfortable or easy. Accepting and living the truth, even when it's painful to do so, gives us our grounding. It enables us to frame our anxieties and our grief, and it gives us a starting point from which progress can be made. Without a grounding in reality, we cannot effectively improve our own well-being or fight climate change. Our grief can show us the depths of our connection to the planet and give us the motivation we need to change.

Grounding Ourselves in Reality

"Curiosity is, in great and generous minds, the first passion and the last."—**Samuel Johnson** (eighteenth-century author)

A few years ago, I went through a health scare. My first instinct when I suspected I was sick was to avoid making the initial medical appointment, as if, somehow, not knowing the truth would change reality. What's better than going through painful treatment, losing my hair, and trading my world as I knew it for a new identity as a sick person? Blissful ignorance! Of course, when somebody else follows this logic, you would point out their failed reasoning and insist they go straight to the doctor. A no-nonsense approach is easier when the "nonsense" isn't your own life experience, when you don't have to face your own fears and distortions. I assumed the worst and avoided the truth, delaying the inevitable and making it worse. I was missing out on the reality, which was that my prognosis wasn't so bad and would have been less bad had I not procrastinated. Had I found my biggest fears came true, I still couldn't have ended up in a place worse than where my mind had already taken me.

The path that we, as a society, have taken in dealing with climate change is similar to my story of delaying inevitable healthcare. Individually, we often handle our fears (about anything, including climate change) by intentionally avoiding the truth. Remember that even bad news helps us put our fears into a healthier perspective. Knowledge can liberate us from the added anxiety of confusion, assumption, and catastrophizing. Ignorance may be bliss, but it is usually short-lived and ultimately detrimental. We can never effectively move forward without knowledge, even if knowing more does bring unpleasant realities to the surface, where we cannot ignore them.

If you have been disheartened by the amount of mental and emotional energy it takes to keep up with climate news, know that you are not alone. Climate change is dynamic and complex. Overwhelm and uncertainty are painful places for us to be, and we prefer to avoid them at all costs. Our brains' favorite avoidance tactic is self-deception. But while denying reality is a common response to a painful truth, it's the worst thing we can do for ourselves and, in this situation, for the planet. On the other hand, fighting climate change—and climate grief—takes bravery, as well as dedication to working through some of our potentially self-sabotaging tendencies.

Sabotaging Reality

"The scares come and go, but everyone likes make-believe monsters to stand in for the real ones."—**Steven King**
(writer, social critic)

The human brain—a dynamic inner world fueled by emotion, reason, and experience—is the powerhouse that created the technologies around us. Thanks to our complex intelligence and rich imagination, we built machines that can figuratively and literally take us anywhere in the world. We found ways to fly, dodge deadly viruses, and create tiny boxes with screens that enable us to do almost anything we want, sitting on our couches. We are capable of growing food in vertical warehouses,[9] creating protein through fermentation,[10] and storing energy from the sun.[11] We have certainly come a long way since our ancestors first figured out simply how to harness other animals to feed them and help them plow.[12] Say what you must about the mess we have made of the planet, we got to this point thanks to ingenuity and innovation.

Yet, remarkable as our brains are, they aren't well equipped to keep up with this complicated outer world we've created. Instead, they are well adapted for another world—the world we evolved with over millennia, the world before the Anthropocene. In the old world, we would have lived in communities of 150 or fewer people and had access to a geographically limited biome. In that world, we would have needed to be able to quickly notice subtle changes in our environment, visually recognize another being as potential friend or foe, decide to fight or flee, and conserve as much mental and physical energy as possible. In a relatively short period of time, we have created a new and convoluted existence involving science, politics, technology, and global relationships—a world in which our old cognitive shortcuts don't cut it. Ultimately, it is only by using our innovative power *wisely* that we will distinguish enterprising progress from chaotic disaster.

I imagine the human brain adapting to the modern world like Mickey Mouse in "The Sorcerer's Apprentice." In this segment of the film *Fantasia* (adapted from a classic Disney book, originally from a poem by Johann Wolfgang von Goethe), Mickey, as the titular apprentice, casts a spell on a mop to do his boring chores. The spell goes awry; soon, there are hundreds of mops flooding and sweeping the room. Things get out of hand as Mickey's attempts to stop the problem create more chaos. Mickey has created something that he assumed he could control, only to discover too late that he cannot.

Our ever-growing modern world of complex technologies, burgeoning population, and conflicting interests and politics has set the stage for the chaos we are now experiencing. Climate change is one of the consequences unleashed by our short-sighted actions, and it is now running a course far greater than most of us could have imagined. Like Mickey the apprentice, those in power aren't utilizing the wisdom of experience to solve humanity's self-inflicted problems. The moral of "The Sorcerer's Apprentice"—that one must respect the learning process and be careful of one's own hubris—is the same as that of countless myths since the Ancient Greeks and Egyptians. We have come a long way technologically, but our age-old biases, hidden and self-sabotaging, remain.

Fight or Flight

In the ancient past, humans developed abilities for quick decision-making, fast action, and intense response to immediate threats. We were a part of the natural food web; we had to be hyper-aware of predators and also of prey. Our decision-making process was linear, and there were few actionable options to escape a threat. We could run, hide, or fight. Our senses could catch subtle changes in the environment; something in the scenery that might not belong would trigger our brains' emergency response system. This system that drove us to the eventual *fight or flight* is our autonomic stress response,[13] something that is still alive and well in our brains, and easily observed in other animals as they freeze, run, cower, or bite when faced with a threat. We can feel this response in our bodies as our hearts race and our faces flush in anxiety-provoking situations. To achieve fast action, the human body responds to a threat with a rush of cortisol, effectively shutting down any unnecessary bodily tasks and directing all available energy to the appropriate physical reaction.

While such a fast reaction was great when we had to escape a predator, in our modern world, it is usually counterproductive. Stressors in today's world usually require thoughtful, solution-oriented strategies rather than an acute, visceral response. They require a more complicated decision-making process and the suspension of immediate gratification. The cortisol released by the autonomic stress response shuts down complex brain functions like critical thinking and emotion regulation, just when we need them most. So, while our brains and bodies still experience the cortisol rush we'd need for fast physical action, we do not use that burst of energy to run or fight. Instead, the excess cortisol hinders us from thinking clearly and fills our bodies with unhealthy stress hormones. Worse still, the long-term effects of this lingering cortisol can include weight gain, anxiety, depression, and more.

This constant struggle between what our brains evolved to do and what modern life requires of us can lead to a host of physical, mental, and emotional symptoms. Fatigue, frustration, hypervigilance, and burnout can surface when we endure prolonged or frequent stress. In particular, those actively involved in social and environmental justice activism consistently experience these symptoms. Indeed, the constant pressure of facing and fighting a long-standing threat makes activists more susceptible to burnout.[14] We cannot run and hide from current global crises, and so, in line with our primitive stress response, our last resort is to freeze. This may be why many of us don't engage in activism in the first place, and why, in times of stress, we find ourselves doing nothing, perhaps even experiencing increased heart rate and blood pressure, having trouble sleeping, and feeling simultaneously jittery and exhausted while stuck in inaction. Even when we are responding to stressors we cannot escape or fix, our bodies would still keep firing up our autonomic stress response in an effort to get us to move away from the anxiety triggers. If we cannot use that energy productively, or at least burn it through physical activity, stress hormones are reabsorbed into our bodies, leaving us worse for the wear.

Cognitive Shortcuts

To outsmart this mechanism, we have to know the tricks our brains use. Biases, mental filters, and heuristics—the shortcuts our brains are so used to taking—were great for a relatively contained environment in which we had to consider only short-term consequences. Following the crowd was smart when strength in numbers kept us from getting ransacked by another group or attacked by a pack of wolves. When we lived in small, isolated, homogenous communities, it was easy and advantageous to spot and rule out even subtle diversity. Indeed, back then, differences in skin tone helped us separate likely relatives from strangers. Unfortunately, that our brains have maintained these archaic thinking patterns, which has produced many highly problematic modern tendencies, of which groupthink and racism are just two examples.[15] Our task now is to retrain our brains to instead slow down, think critically, and make decisions that take into account long-term consequences within an ever-expanding system.

Over time, humankind has continued to view diversity as division, even as population growth increasingly forced us to share space. Our blind preference for the safety of familiarity and our deep-seated biases—based on race, gender, religion, and culture—have provoked world wars, terrorism, and exploitation. One of the worst symptoms of these biases is a lack of empathy, which makes it difficult for us to understand how climate change impacts others—to imagine the effects of rising sea levels if we experienced only the desert, or of desertification if our region remained heavily forested. Even within a given geographical region, those who live in rural settings struggle to empathize with the values and needs of those who live in urban settings, and vice versa. To successfully combat climate change, we have to care about experiences that aren't our own.

Another problematic artifact of our intellectual evolution is a tendency toward all-or-nothing, *binary thinking* whereby everything is either good or bad, black or white. This kind of thinking minimizes our perception of that space in the middle, the "yes, and," the uncomfortable place where there are multiple possibilities and answers. When I was in my mid-twenties, I was told by a much older and wealthier relative that if a person isn't progressive in their twenties, they don't have a heart and if they aren't conservative by their forties, they don't have a brain. I got the message that my hopeful optimism for society was tolerated only because I didn't yet have my own piece of the pie. Since then, I have come to interpret my relative's words as an example of humans' broader struggle to accept that we are a part of an interdependent system. We employ all-or-nothing thinking to simplify our surroundings and therefore our decisions, to more easily justify harming the greater community in the name of self-preservation. Again, back in the day, all-or-nothing, binary thinking, which helped us quickly reach decisions grounded in self-interest, would increase our chance of survival. Now, the same thinking results in dangerously oversimplified, uninformed, and inconsiderate decisions.

So why do we keep the habit? Because our distortions and biases make our clarity-seeking brains feel at ease. Our brains prefer not to entertain anything that might complicate survival or procreation, so it takes conscious effort on our part to prioritize ethical thinking and long-term planning. This is not to say that we cannot exercise these skills or that many among us aren't good at doing so. But we are easily discouraged and tempted to retreat into old habits, even if we know them to be unhealthy, even unethical. The United States' two-party political system is an example of our tendency to strip away complexity in exchange for a sense of certainty. One is forced to pick one political party over the other based on their most important value, and they have little option for dissent even if their other values don't align with the chosen party's platform.

The progressive/conservative dichotomy is disturbing in other ways. It sends the message that it is ignorant to be hopeful and assume change is possible, to be young and have the audacity to buck the status quo. As my wealthy relative suggested, it is smarter to give in, to focus on gathering your own financial resources, and moreover to guard such resources with vehemence as you acquire more. In other words, you would do well to shrink your circle of concern.

Giving up and giving in is a natural tendency across many species. Researchers have conducted many (really quite disturbing) experiments on animals to prove the phenomenon of *learned helplessness*. Humans and nonhumans alike tend to assume, after only a few failed attempts, that an obstacle is insurmountable. We are easily conditioned to expect suffering even if there is an escape. This is why we so readily adjust to or ignore a problem rather than work to fix it. Learned helplessness reduces us to inaction and reliance on the freeze response in the face of stress. It is our tendency toward learned helplessness that, throughout history, has effectively helped usher in unjust economic systems, including capitalism.

A capitalist society like ours is built on the backs of working-class people who are trapped in a system they cannot escape or control; and its existence depends on people with more privilege who *think* they are trapped, unaware of their power to change the system. Life under capitalism teaches us to believe that it is up to us whether we "make it," yet when the vast majority of us inevitably fail, it is because we individually are flawed. Thus, we are caught in an endless cycle of striving and giving up. Capital accumulation is theoretically within reach of anybody, but practically speaking, by design, it is not attainable for all as the system only works when a select few have control of the majority of the resources. And indeed, if we all could get rich, the planet's resources wouldn't be able to keep up with the extra demand. This economic system leaves many of us vulnerable, never feeling like we have "enough," scared to share the resources we do manage to secure, and pressured by a scarcity mentality. This collective learned helplessness is silently undermining our potential to create meaningful cultural growth, as well as progress that could be leading us to a sustainable future.

Our tendency to give up and accept what we perceive to be out of our control affects our motivation to learn. The hardest class I took in college was physics, which quickly became intimidating enough that I struggled just to show up to class. I was so reluctant to go that I was on time for that class exactly once during the entire semester. Much of math and science gave me the same feeling throughout high school and college. I had a *fixed mindset* about my ability to learn: I either knew something or didn't, and I didn't dare push myself to take a risk and possibly fail. These kind of fears might be why many opt not to think about personal shortcomings, the flaws in our economic system, or the realities of climate change. If we feel a problem is beyond our grasp, we are intimidated by the thought of trying to solve it. It's much easier to ignore or accept that problem as a matter of fact, which is sometimes a healthy course of action. Other times, we render ourselves helpless when what we really need to do is fight.

We may also extend our understanding of learned help-lessness to the *black box metaphor*, which suggests that we tend to interpret complicated phenomena as composed of a logical beginning and a conclusion, with an unknown process in the middle (like the inside of a black box). Examples include product assembly, food processing, car production, engineering design projects, the creation of a music album—anything with a process few understand. Components go in, something recognizable comes out; what happens in between is ambiguous. Many of us comprehend climate change this way. We don't know exactly *how*, but we understand simply that we are burning fossil fuels and that doing so is causing a global temperature rise. That is enough for some to accept the concept of climate change and for others to deny it. If we don't understand the mechanisms of climate change, it's easy to be misled and to become susceptible to logical fallacies. Without enough foundational knowledge to be able to scrutinize the information we consume, we tend to accept things that at first glance seem logical but turn out to be false. Once, I told a student to wait to make up her mind until she had more information. She asked, "Will I ever have enough information to decide once and for all?" While one's core values tend to remain stable and shape their identity, their decisions and interpretations of the world are healthiest when they are malleable. We should always be willing to push ourselves to learn, be ready to exercise critical thinking, and stay open to changing our minds if new evidence is strong.

Sometimes, we are willing to settle on an explanation even *without* a logical conclusion. Our brains are so desperate to decide and move on that when we don't have a good answer, we subscribe to a myth. We tend to engage in *magical thinking*, believing that we can influence the outcome of something that is out of our control. When the Black Death was ravaging Europe, killing about one third of the population, people assumed that they were being punished by a supernatural force and that the only way to escape was to win their god's favor. Thus, to protect themselves, they did all sorts of things that were not at all helpful, including flagellation and even human sacrifice. In COVID-19 times, despite the existence of solid science to explain bacteria and viruses, and the benefits of good hygiene, religion still had a huge influence on how some people interpreted the pandemic. The workings of gods have remained a common explanation for the ills of the world even as we uncover compelling evidence suggesting otherwise. Myths are attractive when they give us a sense of certainty. All too often, we trade unsettling truth for comforting fiction.

Retraining Our Brains

"Twenty-five years ago, people could be excused for not knowing much, or doing much, about climate change. Today, we have no excuse."—**Desmond Tutu** (former archbishop of Cape Town)

It is easy to default to our biases and habit of binary thinking, thus falling victim to learned helplessness and logical fallacies. On the other hand, challenging these ingrained patterns takes effort. The most inspiring change-makers among us are those who keep learning and changing as they learn. They refuse to preserve a problematic status quo. The most inspiring change-makers among us fight against inherent biases and distortions to instead see the whole system, to understand processes and phenomena beyond what affects them personally. They explore the complexity of the forces affecting their reality. They are admirable because to retrain one's brain to work toward personal growth and keep challenging one's beliefs is a big undertaking. I have always been inspired by the story of Aldo Leopold, an early naturalist and conservationist famous for writing *A Sand County Almanac* and referred to by many as the father of wildlife ecology. In the early 1900s, he worked in the Southwest to rid the ecosystem of wolves to maintain populations of deer for men to hunt. After decades of faulty reasoning, he realized that he had been gravely wrong and that wolves played a critically important role in the ecosystem, and spent the rest of his life acknowledging his wrongdoing and educating others.[16]

The prefrontal cortex is the part of the human brain most responsible for coping, empathy, planning, and *systems thinking*.[17] Note, though, that this part of the brain isn't even fully developed until one is well into their twenties. Our job as decent humans is to act according to what is in the best interest of not just ourselves but also others—our families and our communities. According to what we know about prefrontal cortex development, this may be more difficult to do until one reaches their mid-twenties; by then, however, one may have established other values that are antithetical to community living. I wonder how, in a culture that rewards wealth building and individual autonomy, we can shift our values to prioritize the types of growth that are actually important for our future, such as improvements in the accessibility of healthcare and education.

In what ways have we gone off track? The world may be more complicated as a whole, but for many of us, life is safer and more predictable compared to past generations. Many of us enjoy the privilege of consistent shelter, abundant drinking water, access to food, community, romance, laziness, and leisure. Without the stress of constantly struggling to meet basic needs, we have time to play, create, and help others. We could assume this freedom has made us a smarter, healthier, happier species. We could assume that our own needs having been met, it is easy for us to give back to the community. That might be so, and some of us do give back. But there is no conclusive evidence suggesting we are happier or smarter than our ancestors, and despite modern advances in healthcare, we have gotten unhealthier by several measures.[18] As far as helping others, there may actually be an inverse relationship between how much we have and how much we are willing to share.[19] We have created a world of entertainment, comfort, and choice, yet these added benefits may not have yielded net-positive returns. As a consequence of our culture of seeking leisure and affluence, we are under constant stress, as if we were still merely meeting basic needs. We are just as competitive and divided as ever. The psychological pain of chasing after impossible measures of success mirrors the damage we cause, thanks to our uncurbed demands, to the planet and to others. As we push ourselves to accomplish more, to achieve the unachievable, we push the planet to produce well beyond what's sustainable.

We think we act with accuracy and in a way that's logical and measured, but there is still much for us to learn about the world and ourselves. What to us is a mystery likely has logical explanations that we haven't yet uncovered. At this point in time, only a small percentage of the ocean has been explored, species previously unknown to humans are discovered all the time, and weather is still difficult to predict. Paleontologists continue digging up skeletons of strange, fantastical animals. The human brain contains as many mysteries for us to solve as does the world around us, and psychology, one of the newer sciences, is also brimming with new findings. Now, in the face of global climate change, we realize that we have never created the tools for dealing with this type of problem.

This doesn't mean we don't have the capacity to solve climate change. We do. We have the ability to rise to the occasion. There are people among us with the intelligence and wisdom to lead the way. After all, we as a species managed to come up with both science and social justice. It will take a healthy dose of modesty for us to retrain our brains. We must be willing to become students again. The smartest people in any field will tell you how much they have yet to uncover. Einstein allegedly said, "The more I learn, the more I realize how much I don't know." This is true for climate experts as they work to predict interactions in an extremely complex system. Still, as experts, they have a far better grasp of the subject matter than we do. Yet, we can confuse our own strong opinions as knowledge; susceptible to the spread of misinformation, we may even come to believe our wishful thinking and close ourselves off from deeper learning and from other interpretations. Our egos and fears distort our perceptions. During the COVID-19 pandemic, as we saw people with little knowledge about the science of viruses wield loud, ever-present voices influencing their hordes of followers, it became increasingly difficult to know which narrative to believe. By contrast, people who gave their opinions with care and with few absolutes were probably the ones worth listening to.

Remember that people are flawed and that our flawed, binary thought patterns tend to be stubborn and reactionary. Our brains sacrifice accuracy for a quickly formed best guess. We are hardwired to make shortcuts via cognitive biases and heuristics when we need a quick solution, so much so that these biases and heuristics seep into our thinking even when we aren't in a hurry to make up our minds. They can also make us short-sighted and selfish. While we can easily spot these gaps in logic in other people, it is hard to recognize them in ourselves. Once great as survival mechanisms, these cognitive tendencies fall short in our current world. We did evolve to be able to quickly learn a bunch of tricks to manipulate the world around us; now, we've changed it forever. We were never a perfect species, and hopefully we have much more evolving to accomplish in our future.

Keeping Reality in Perspective

Navigating climate change and climate grief is a long-term journey. Panicking won't help. A total sacrifice of your livelihood won't help. Nihilism won't solve anything or feel good in the end. Humanity has encountered a myriad of crises in the time that humans have been alive, and as we advance, so do our problems. If you want to feel pessimistic, you need only look at our response to climate change so far, which can put things in a rather harsh perspective. Personally, I'd rather believe we as a global community can learn how to step up to the challenge, collaborate, and survive, even thrive. To get there, we need a more critical understanding of not just the world around us but also our inner worlds. That is our first, most important step.

Give yourself grace and space to learn more as you go, to make mistakes when you have to, and to say simply that you do not know. It's time we normalize acknowledging our own limits and making room for growth, and supporting experts in doing the same. You do not need to become a climate expert to advocate sustainability and mitigate climate change. Focus on your values and what you envision for the future. Let yourself enjoy the journey of learning.

Start with the very simple grounding exercise of evaluating some of your own observations. It's hard to comprehend climate change without paying attention to changes in the weather, this being most easily achieved by collecting and recording data. To strengthen your own observation skills, consider the natural place you know the best. If you grew up in a specific region or have lived in a neighborhood for a number of years, you can find observable phenomena that will help you see change over time. Notice when certain plants start to grow or bloom each year, or how the water levels in a pond change. Record this data and continue adding to it each week, month, year. Find your neighborhood elders and ask them what they've observed. You will find that subtle yet important changes in your local ecosystem can tell a more overarching story, one that you aren't accustomed to hearing. Indeed, it became a lot easier for me to grasp climate science when I could see symptoms of climate change in my own backyard.

Climate Change 101

"Do the best you can until you know better. Then, when you know better, do better."—**Maya Angelou** (legendary poet, scholar, civil rights activist)

For most of us, it's been a long time since our last Earth science lesson. Maybe your last science class was before climate change started to be included in textbooks (although in many school districts, omitting climate change from the curriculum is still the standard). It's easy to be misguided by common misunderstandings about climate change if we do not have at least some foundational knowledge, but the mechanisms behind climate change are not so mysterious once we familiarize ourselves with the science. Below is a possible starting point—questions frequently asked by my students and friends and topics they find confusing. I am no expert, and each niche topic attracts its own researchers who know far more than any layperson, so please use this as a launching point for your own learning. Some easily accessible and reliable resources to start with include publications by National Geographic, the National Oceanic and Atmospheric Administration (NOAA), and the United Nations Environment Programme.

Carbon

The first common misunderstanding about carbon is that we are creating carbon, and since plants use it anyway, more carbon is okay. The reality is that carbon levels on Earth do not change; carbon merely travels back and forth between the planet and its atmosphere. We are shifting carbon around, currently at an unprecedented pace. The fourth most abundant element in the universe, carbon is abundant even in our bodies, accounting for nearly 20 percent of our body weight. It is required for the creation of DNA as well as protein, and therefore all life forms. The carbon cycle is the constant flux of carbon being released into the atmosphere and reabsorbing into *carbon sinks*—rocks, sediments, and living things. When we burn fossil fuels, we are releasing carbon—we are redistributing carbon, not creating more. We don't produce or destroy carbon. We have no method to remove carbon from the planet, nor would we want to, as it is a basic building block for all life on Earth.

Climate change is caused by rapid carbon movement that destabilizes the carbon cycle as it interacts with the water cycle. Carbon sinks, where carbon is stored, are an important part of the cycle; of these, trees are probably the best known. They store the carbon they take in while releasing oxygen. A tree continues collecting more carbon while alive and remains a carbon sink even after it falls, slowly releasing the carbon as it decomposes. A tree that is burned releases carbon into the atmosphere. There is a finite amount of this element that a tree can store, and how much it can absorb in a specified period of time depends on many factors, from its local ecosystem to its growth rate. There are other carbon sinks that are more important than trees. Our oceans' algae, like kelp and phytoplankton, store more carbon than trees do. Whales, the largest living animal, are also significant carbon sinks. We effectively turn stored carbon into carbon that can actively influence its surroundings when we manipulate rocks and living organisms and release the carbon they were holding.

Carbon takes the form of CO_2 (carbon dioxide) when it is released into the atmosphere, where it plays an important role in heat absorption. It may be absorbed by a living organism on land, or it may be absorbed into the ocean. While rocks account for the most carbon storage, carbon absorption into rocks is an extremely slow process. Ideally, living organisms absorb carbon and use it to create more oxygen, protein, and DNA. However, the more the planet's surface is converted into spaces void of living organisms, the less carbon can be absorbed. This is one reason why deforestation is a significant problem. Most carbon dioxide is absorbed into the ocean. While carbon is healthy for the ocean and easily absorbed by different forms of sea life, too much carbon too fast results in that carbon having nowhere to go, making the ocean more acidic. This means the CO_2 is staying in the water, reducing the water's pH level. The rate of ocean acidification today is from ten to a whopping one hundred times what it has been at any time over the past 55 million years.[20] One of the biggest effects of ocean acidification is on calcifying organisms like corals and shellfish. Small shelled creatures play a critical role in the food web, serving as food for countless other organisms, including large mammals. A reduction in these small animals' numbers results in a trophic cascade, or ecosystem collapse.

At first glance, it may seem that while ocean acidification due to excess carbon is bad, terrestrial carbon sequestration can be a good thing for forests. However, organisms like trees need more than carbon dioxide to thrive. They also need water, nutrients in the soil, and the amount of sunlight their species has adapted to over the course of evolution. The water cycle works in tandem with the carbon cycle to maintain a relative balance that has existed on this planet since the last major extinction event 65 million years ago. Now that weather patterns are changing, the resulting planet-wide water redistribution is affecting forests. Industrial agricultural practices are stripping soils of nutrients, and contaminated water is carrying pollutants far and wide. All of this further weakens both terrestrial and marine ecosystems.

Weather and Climate

Another common misunderstanding is that cold weather proves global warming isn't real, isn't so bad, or is getting better. The reality is that cold weather in a given location does not suggest anything about overall global climate change, as localized weather patterns are, metaphorically speaking, a mere sentence in a long story. A recent president would famously laugh off global warming as a hoax whenever the weather was cold. This is an example of not considering the entire system and not appreciating the many factors that affect climate. Climate change isn't like a light switch. Canada wouldn't suddenly have mild winters like Mexico. But what we can see are noticeable patterns over time.

The climate change we currently experience is an increase in extreme weather events, which are caused by an overall global warming trend. One reason for this causal relationship is that warmer air leads to stronger storms. Hurricanes, tornadoes, and lightning storms are all heat-related, as heat causes faster evaporation and more moisture in the atmosphere. An increase in the moisture available to be released in a storm leads to higher precipitation, and thus more floods and mudslides.

Meanwhile, storm surge—water being pushed toward the shore from the ocean during a storm—adds to the rise in sea levels. Sea level rise is caused partly by melting polar ice and partly by the increase in water volume, as warmer water has more volume compared to colder water. Warming in the two Poles is changing jet stream patterns, causing some places to experience colder weather than normal, but when we look at the global average, there is a rapid and clear trend toward warmer weather. Overall, we are experiencing more heat records than cold records; we are seeing both warmer nights and warmer days.

To notice changes in weather patterns, it is best to record these patterns and make comparisons over time rather than rely on personal, day-to-day memory.

Cyclical Phenomena

Many people falsely believe that climate change and mass extinction are both a normal, cyclical part of life on Earth. The reality is that the present climate change event is an unnatural phenomenon, and based on geological evidence, it does not fit the pattern of Earth's previous cycles. This is not the first time carbon has impacted climate enough to cause mass extinction—it's the sixth—but this is the first time such an event has progressed at such a fast pace. Even in previous events of mass carbon release, such as from numerous super volcano eruptions, mass extinction occurred over several hundreds or thousands of years. In comparison, humans have significantly altered carbon distribution in just the last 150 years, and since 1970, we have already observed a more than two-thirds drop in biodiversity. Measurements of the carbon released from industrial practices tell us beyond doubt that this mass extinction is happening faster than all such events in the past and will only continue accelerating. Mass extinctions in the past were not caused by natural cycles; there have always been identifiable catalysts behind cooling and warming trends. Significant swings in how much carbon is stored versus how much is in the environment are caused by major tectonic or extraterrestrial events. During most periods of global cooling or warming in the past, we were at the mercy of volcanoes, sometimes even asteroids. Ecosystems have long been in battle with nonliving forces of nature; living organisms willfully causing climate change is unprecedented.

Then and Now: Mass Extinction Events

Theories suggest that the first mass extinction event, 440 million years ago, was caused by a loss of CO_2 in the atmosphere. The increase in marine life in a world mostly covered in water was what took CO_2 from the air, cooling the earth and causing glaciation and a drop in sea levels. This shrank the habitat necessary for the majority of life on the planet, causing the extinction of nearly 90 percent of all species.

Then, about 365 million years ago, another CO_2 imbalance caused about three quarters of life on Earth to go extinct. The plants that had evolved to live on land after the last extinction event began to root deeply into the ground, sending nutrients into the surrounding seas. This increase in nutrients in the water sparked algae blooms, which sucked oxygen out of the water, suffocating marine life.

The third and worst mass extinction occurred about 252 million years ago, when atmospheric CO_2 shot up due to volcanic activity in Siberia. Bacteria that thrive on CO_2 began to multiply, releasing more methane into the air. The combination of these two gasses caused warming and acidification of both the air and the water. This increase in CO_2 and methane millions of years ago and what is occurring today are very similar, despite the causes being very different. The fourth mass extinction, around 210 million years ago, seems to have been similar to the third, with either volcanic activity or an asteroid causing entrapment of CO_2 in the atmosphere, thus warming the planet.

Finally came the fifth extinction event, the one we know to have caused the extinction of dinosaurs. This event happened 66 million years ago and was likely caused by a temperature drop when an asteroid hit the earth and debris in the air blocked sunshine.

Today, as we are witnessing rapid and severe species extinction for the sixth time, it is happening faster than ever before. And because we can measure the rate of exhaust emission from industry, we know that human behavior is the cause of most of the carbon released into the atmosphere.

Two Degrees

What is the use of a house if you haven't got a tolerable planet to put it on?"—**Henry David Thoreau** (naturalist, poet, philosopher)

A misunderstanding particularly common in the United States is that a global temperature rise of two degrees is not significant. The reality is that just a two-degree increase will have catastrophic consequences. Because we see temperature highs and lows that are far more than two degrees apart every day, it may seem that two degrees would hardly make a noticeable difference. While this may be true for humans, who are accustomed to life in shelters, even a smaller change in average temperatures will already upend the seasons' timelines, impacting migration and therefore reproduction in migrating species. An inconsistent heating pattern affects which foods are available on a typical migration route; as such, it may shorten routes or make the journey unsurvivable for birds, fishes, and other animals. Moreover, the slightest temperature change (of less than a degree) can exacerbate drying soil and melting ice; it would impact lake water evaporation, the urban heat index, and resulting precipitation patterns in every region of the globe.

In some areas, the effects of this seemingly minor global temperature increase of two degrees Celsius are already clearly felt. The Poles, home to ice sheets and glaciers, have experienced days of record heat, contributing to more of the ice melting. Besides its contribution to sea level rise, melting ice also releases more stored carbon and methane into the atmosphere. Remember that two degrees Celsius and two degrees Fahrenheit are very different. To put things into perspective, those who use Fahrenheit should imagine an additional two to three degrees of heat.

A Race against Time?

It is nice to assume that we will still have time to make adjustments once we see more of the impacts of climate change. This assumption wastes precious time. Climate change can be thought of like an illness. Once we experience symptoms, it is too late to avoid getting sick. My clients and friends frequently talk about their worry that we are running out of time to act, and they are right to worry. Climate change is like compounding interest. A little bit, with time, can go a long way when we're dealing with exponential growth. In normal times, the base rate of extinction would be 10 percent of total species every million years. In most of the mass extinctions to date, the planet has lost more than 75 percent of species over the span of two million years; in comparison, faster extinction events happened over thousands of years. Today, we are losing species at a rate somewhere between one hundred to more than one thousand times faster than ever before. Early *Homo sapiens* hunted animals such as wooly mammoths, ground sloths, and moas to extinction; they also likely drove the other early human species to go extinct through violence and resource competition. The rate of continuing extinction is extremely hard to predict, and it is likely that many of our measurements are underestimates. What is clear is that our time to respond to climate change is running out, and the longer we wait, the worse the outcome is sure to be.

The potential for climate change mitigation and adaptation shrinks as more carbon is released and biodiversity declines. To reverse climate change, we need carbon to be absorbed. Carbon sequestration happens over time and requires a variety of life forms at mature stages. Trees and other plants, algae, and animals all take time to grow big or numerous enough to sequester significant amounts of carbon.

None of the accepted estimations on climate change timelines suggests that we can wait another generation to make drastic changes. Each time we negatively affect an ecosystem by cutting into it, heating it up, dumping a chemical in its water, or polluting it with noise, we are destabilizing it further. Even our best estimates cannot take every possible factor into consideration, so we do not know exactly at what point the planet would become uninhabitable for humans. What we know is that today, scientists working on various disparate studies all report similar findings: alarmingly unstable conditions in nearly every ecosystem on the planet.

Humans' Adaptability

"It is difficult to get a man to understand something, when his salary depends upon his not understanding it."
—**Upton Sinclair** (writer, political activist)

What is particularly troubling is that some of us believe humans can adapt to a hotter planet with less biodiversity. But even if we could adapt, would we want to? Imagine living in a world without nature as we know it. Countless sci-fi movies have explored our potential futures in a dystopian, AI-governed, metallic world void of trees and sunlight.[21] Scientists and sci-fi authors alike continue to speculate on how we would adapt if any variety of environmental loss occurs. Can we mechanize food production to the point where we don't even need nature itself? Can we create a system in which we don't need the bees to pollinate plants or the soil to store and transfer nutrients? With the creation of AI and the sheer rate at which it is surpassing human capacities, we are in for many surprises in the coming years. Considering that cell phones weren't anticipated until just a few years prior to their invention, we can bet we are headed for a future far beyond any stretch of our imagination. So, sure, maybe humans can adapt—learn to feed ourselves and keep ourselves alive on a planet void of the Mother Nature we've always known. The question then might be: should we, or do we want to, live in a world without nature?

The mental health repercussions for humans living in a completely mechanized world are likely immense; the grief from losing our natural home would be unimaginable. This doesn't even take into account the pain of having to sacrifice our ethics when we destroy entire species of plants and animals. There aren't many people, not even the world's richest, rallying for a future without nature. Even those who predict it will happen, who are creating AI software and exploring mechanized food production and life in a sterile bubble, are not celebrating. It is difficult to fathom such an unnatural world, but when we talk about adapting after mass extinction, an unnatural world is exactly what we would be dealing with. Maybe humans can adapt to a post–mass extinction world. But just how far are we willing to go? Why focus on adapting while we can still work to avoid such a dystopia?

The toll climate change takes on humanity will be just as stark as its toll on the rest of the ecosystem. Humans' sources of water, air, and food are all receding or becoming too polluted for safe consumption. This reality is already obvious to many, especially in the Global South, on low-lying islands, in coastal areas, in areas of drought or flooding, and in urban food deserts. Technology and innovation provide us with a false sense of security. Regardless of our technological advances, we will likely always be subject to the basic rules of life, as will any other carbon-, oxygen-, and water-reliant species on this planet. It is unclear at this point what the world will be like in thirty, sixty, or a hundred years. I hope that rather than wonder whether we will adapt, more people will focus on what can be done so we don't have to adapt.

Won't Somebody Fix the Problem?

There is no quick fix to climate change because it is a multifaceted issue. Throughout human history, societies that grew mighty enough in size and capabilities to create governments and economies and to enjoy leisure time but that no longer exist tended to be wiped out by the same factors at play today. For many societies of the past, climate change amplified destructive habits that led to conflict and war, deforestation, overpopulation, and unsustainable resource use. The people of Rapa Nui, known as Easter Island, were one well-known example of a society that likely brought about its own demise by clearcutting the island, weakening defenses against raiders and colonizers, and ultimately causing climate change. Already an unstable society, the Mississippian culture, which covered much of the current-day United States' Midwestern states, was also pushed over the edge by climate change and accompanying food insecurity.

We seem unable or unwilling to acknowledge our impact on the environment or on others, choosing instead to focus on short-term gains. Of course, we are *capable* of managing our consumption, lightening our impact, and behaving compassionately toward others. Yet, if history is any indication, we have a long-standing tendency toward resource hoarding, unchecked consumption, and unsustainable growth, against the warnings of the wise among us. We tell ourselves that there must surely be enough smart people, somewhere, who are creating the very solutions we need; but this only means we have all watched too many superhero movies.

Part of the issue is that we are not really a "we." Even if somebody could save us, wouldn't they save their country first? Their company? Their political party? What would be their bottom line? And from whom should they protect themselves? Ironically, in a period of abundant technology and opportunity, we also feel intense fears toward others, driven by self-preservation. Self-preservation is important, but where is the line between survival and selfishness? Why haven't we outgrown this instinct when we have made so much progress in making our lives easier? We have created a culture that rewards selfishness in the name of capital accumulation, individual achievement, autonomy, and career success. Indeed, our hardwired tendency toward self-preservation might just be working against the progress we think we are making. In a world where those of us with resources can keep acquiring more, we continue to value competition over community. Instead of collectively solving pressing problems, we prioritize personal gains. Philanthropy becomes an exclusive hobby, while social justice work oftentimes comes with social ostracization and personal hardship. Fighting for social justice means fighting against age-old tendencies toward selfishness. If we look a little more closely into the dark sides of capitalism and how difficult it is to live a life that challenges capitalist society, we would see just how inherently anti-sustainability our current economic and political systems are,[22] in which our desire for individual capital renders us frozen in our own self-interested pursuits even as we face climate change. We cannot fight climate change if we hold on to these values. We have to prioritize community and be willing to take a long hard look at our own lifestyles and desires. The "somebody" we are looking for to save humanity is staring back at all of us in the mirror.

Can Individuals Effect Change?

Also common yet detrimental is the defeatist belief that there is nothing an individual can do about our climate anyway, so there is no point in trying. The reality is that whether one can do little or a lot does not change the fact that doing *nothing* is the worst option. Indeed, fighting climate change may feel like an impossible endeavor. It is true that any individual's direct contribution to climate change through choices made in their day-to-day life is miniscule when we think about large corporations allowed to release massive amounts of carbon into the air, with the government's blessing. The largest contributors to climate change include plastics, deforestation, animal agriculture, and fossil fuel burning. While corporations and governments hold the most responsibility for climate change and thus could catalyze the most progress in combatting it, individual change is important too. To deal with climate change effectively, we have to understand how it was driven by societal evolution toward capitalism and how we might reverse course by dramatically reducing our consumption of fossil fuels, natural resources, and other animals. We are the ones who created the current systems; ultimately, we have the power to change them. The more people believe that, the more change we will see. Change at the local level inspires change at the regional and national levels, and there are plenty of success stories. Ease your self-doubt and renew your sense of self-empowerment by consuming stories that inspire rather than tuning to typical news outlets, which focus only on whatever is most dramatic.

Demystifying the complex aspects of climate change is an important first step in understanding what we risk—and what we grieve—as we move forward toward climate solutions. Remember that unlike with the five previous major extinction events, this time, climate change can be manipulated. This epoch of history is not being driven by a cascade of uncontrollable forces of nature; we determine the outcome, as our actions will lead to either further complications or solutions, to either more problems or adaptation strategies. Yes, we *will* continue to see climate migration and an influx of climate refugees. Desertification and increased wildfires and flooding *will* make many highly populated regions uninhabitable. Conflicts over water and other resources will become more prevalent. I am not writing this to patronize you or inject scientifically unfounded hope. But we *do* still have control over the ultimate outcome. We can rein in and reverse habits that contribute to deforestation, pollution, and exploitation. There are many feasible solutions to a range of climate problems; the main issue, then, is that we do not yet have or know how to harness the social power to overcome our selfish motivations and to force politicians and corporations to change. But this is a cultural issue, and culture can change quickly.

Truth will inform cultural change if critical thinking and action are encouraged, even expected, instead of apathy and learned helplessness. Review the science of climate change so you can feel more confident in dispelling myths and clarifying ambiguous concepts for yourself and others. Each time you see an article with a clickbait or sensationalized headline, slow down, check the sources, and take the time to understand it instead of relying solely on intuition and wishful thinking. Intellectualizing climate change will help you build your coping strategies and action plans. The truth will set you free from damaging myths, along with the unnecessary stress and misleading anxieties. All big changes start with individuals.

2
GETTING TO KNOW CLIMATE GRIEF

"The reality is that you will grieve forever. You will not
'get over' the loss of a loved one; you will learn to live
with it. You will heal and you will rebuild yourself around
the loss you have suffered. You will be whole again but
you will never be the same. Nor should you be the same,
nor would you want to."—**Elisabeth Kübler-Ross**
(psychiatrist, pioneer in near-death studies)

The grief we feel about climate change is a reasonable, rational
reaction to living in an increasingly unhealthy environment.
Grief itself is a process of emotions that transitions us from the
reality we previously lived in to the new reality after a loss or
change. Like any other kind of grief, climate grief affects us as
we experience the loss of, or the threat of losing, an important
part of our lives. Climate grief can be triggered by trauma from
extreme events such as hurricanes, wildfires, and drought or by
the ambiguity of gradual change. Not knowing how bad things
will be or how much time we have before the worst occurs can

lead to our feeling powerless, fearful, exhausted, and burned out. We know for a fact that climate change takes an emotional toll on those directly suffering its consequences, including extreme weather events, food scarcity, and so on; but those of us who learn about climate change from afar are also affected emotionally. We feel grief flickering in and out of our focus as we hear one bad news after another, taking in the harsh indifference of Mother Nature and reflecting on the moral failings of our species.

The concept of the grieving process was framed by Elisabeth Kübler-Ross in 1969 in her first book, *On Death and Dying*. Kübler-Ross identified the process by its five stages: denial, anger, bargaining, sadness, and acceptance. Grief itself is not a choice, according to Kübler-Ross, but we can manage our responses to it. Ultimately, we adapt best when we consciously experience and work with each stage of grief. Awareness and effort allow us to move through the process, all the while learning about ourselves and our needs and letting ourselves more fully heal from loss. Being aware of grief, consciously experiencing it, and reflecting on it help us cope and become more resilient.

We humans are not simply machines that react predictably to triggers in our surroundings. Our emotional lives are highly complex. We interact with each other, the natural world around us, and our own moods and circumstances using a sense of perception that constantly evolves. The stories we carry with us about who we are and what we are capable of are highly influenced both by others and by memories, connections, and the delicate balance of chemicals in our brains. For as different as we are, we all experience the world around us with the same range of general emotions. While each of us is an individual with unique experiences, the emotional needs and fears we have in common make us far more alike than different, even across divides of values and beliefs. We all want to feel safe and secure, and we all use similar tools to fulfill those needs.

We all experience grief throughout life, both in obviously difficult times and during seemingly insignificant events. Grief is what we feel when a disruption in our lives results in a need to change some or all aspects of our lifestyles, our identities, or our expectations for the future. Leaving something behind or being left behind (even when change is ultimately for the best) provokes grief. It can be isolating, upsetting, frustrating, and potentially impairing; provided that we are healthy and resilient, we can generally work through it and come out the other side with a renewed sense of normalcy. By "normalcy," I mean that we can resume previous pursuits of pleasure, productivity, community, and whatever else used to define our lives, even as we live with an enduring scar or a new purpose.

Grief is more an automatic reaction to change than a conscious response. All grief tends to follow a universal pattern of core emotions as one adapts to a new life after loss. Climate grief is no exception. The purpose of grief is simple: to ease the brain into a new reality through steps that help maintain some sense of control and well-being. The process of grief is a complex dance between the feeling brain and the thinking brain, between the present, the past, and the future, between reality and wishful thinking, until we move on and feel settled again. Still, the harsher the new reality, the stronger the grief. Grieving is an ongoing process and can indeed keep us locked in a stronghold for the rest of our lives.

The stages of grief each play a role in protecting our well-being and self-preservation as we grieve. Though the process is rarely linear, these stages are generally experienced in the order as follows:

- Denial: We deny reality or overlook parts of the truth because we are not ready to handle it in its entirety. Loss can be so traumatizing that the conscious brain is not yet equipped to process it, so it works extra hard to block the trauma out.

- Anger: We get angry and project blame onto another thing or person as the source of that anger, in order to mask our vulnerability—our actual feelings of sadness, loneliness, or guilt. Anger acts as a buffer between what happened and how vulnerable the event makes us feel.

- Bargaining: We try to come up with some way to change the situation or regain a sense of control. We ruminate over what-ifs, or we make a deal with ourselves or a higher power in hopes that the situation will be different if we can prove we've learned our lesson.

- Sadness: Finally, deep despair grips us as we realize the truth is not going to change and feel the gravity of the new reality. Also referred to as "depression," this is the stage at which we access our unmasked emotions.

- Acceptance: Here, we give in to reality rather than fight it, and we integrate our loss into a new emotional and physical routine. Accepting that it is time to refocus and make new plans lets us move forward toward renewed health.

At any point throughout the grieving process, a memory, situation, or bad day may induce emotions and toss us back into phases we already moved through. Grieving is an ongoing, messy, difficult, and often lifelong task. While the above framework captures the typical feelings we would go through, there is not a set period of time for each stage, nor a set number of times it should be repeated. How we experience and move through grief depends on our ability to feel and show vulnerability, along with the tools and resources we have at our disposal to support our mental health. The more deeply we loved what we lost, the less likely that we will ever get a sense that we have "graduated" or moved on from our grief. That's typical, even good. I've come to appreciate the enduring tinge of sadness that occasionally passes through my mind when I think about past losses. I see it as a reminder of how valuable something or someone I loved has been in building my current identity.

The college I attended for my undergraduate degree had endured a tragic tornado a few years before my class entered. A child in the town had died and many buildings had been destroyed in the storm. By the time I began my freshman year, trees had been replanted, memorials had been constructed, and day-to-day talk of the storm had quieted. Ceremonies marked five years, then a decade, since the event. Trees grew, businesses recovered, and the fabric of the community grew stronger around the stitching of its grief. But on each anniversary and during each tornado watch, the tension in the town was palpable as the memory of the tornado came roaring back up to the surface of the community's collective psyche. It taught me to see my own grief as a resident in my mind, something I would come to live with and learn from. We don't have a choice other than to accept that the loss that is the source of grief will change us. We can let the loss itself define us, or we can take away lessons from the experience.

Since you're reading this book, this topic likely resonates with you and you are likely experiencing sadness, fear, or confusion in the face of climate change. You may have moved through such emotions in the past, but this grief may feel very different.

The very threat of climate change is so all-encompassing that our psychological tools for survival and coping may be coming up short, leaving some of us with intolerable anxiety. Thus, the concept of grief may seem unfitting. On the other hand, to those who aren't immersed in climate science or current events, the idea of climate grief may seem premature or inappropriate. This dichotomy leads those of us who do feel climate grief to wonder if we should feel embarrassment over our sensitivity or anger at those who don't share the emotional burden.

When we as a society experience grief, we tend to race to action to fix the problem. Memorials, restorations, consumer-driven economic initiatives, policy changes, and holidays are some of the ways in which we have collectively responded to local or national tragedies in the past. Grief is personal; not everybody moves along at the same pace, and no community response has ever left each individual feeling understood and represented. Global issues do not impact us uniformly, as we each act based on a unique history, level of resilience, experience with traumas, and access to resources.

Here are just a few of the factors that differ between one individual and the next that affect response to climate change: whether one sees climate change in daily life; whether climate change directly impacts one's livelihood; whether one is educated enough or has enough information to understand climate science; whether one's social surroundings and community values encourage acceptance of climate change; and whether one is generally resilient against trauma. All of these factors determine whether we are more or less likely to be open to accepting and adapting to the reality of climate change.

One truth has become clear to me as I looked at the climate crisis through the lens of grief: *everybody is grieving climate change*.

This may seem implausible when we constantly hear vehement arguments against its existence. Denial is, after all, the first stage of grief, and remembering this helps build our compassion as we all are experiencing different stages of grief at any given time and are expressing grief in different ways.

Stages of Grief

"The most beautiful people we have known are those who have known defeat, known suffering, known struggle, known loss, and have found their way out of the depths. These persons have an appreciation, a sensitivity, and an understanding of life that fills them with compassion, gentleness, and a deep loving concern. Beautiful people do not just happen."—**Elisabeth Kübler-Ross** (psychiatrist, pioneer in near-death studies)

Nobody chooses to go through grief, and we don't always recognize it when it is happening. Nevertheless, most of the instances of grief we endure do have discernible sources, and at some point, we begin to identify what we are going through. Often, when we finally reach acceptance is when we can, with confidence, say that we have been grieving, as we now feel strong enough to blend the grieving process with other aspects of life. We may start talking about the impact of grief and our loss, or we may be more comfortable mentioning the loss in passing in general conversation. As time goes on, we can talk about other things or do fun activities, which previously may have induced guilt; we can get through a day without the loss being at the front of our minds. Eventually, we can talk to others about our loss more freely, without strong emotions bubbling to the surface.

The passing of time, combined with reflection and productive coping, has brought us to a point where our loss is manageable.

Though rarely linear, the stages of grief show us how the brain processes a loss or change, with well-being being its basic objective. In the case of devastating loss, enduring grief may be a more laborious task. Grief from smaller changes—or changes that can be tackled with the help of a lot of tools and support—is easier to bear. Whether a person grieves "well" is dependent on the impact of the change, as well as the resources and capacities they have to face the grief itself. As we will see, there are plenty of reasons why some people never really start grieving but choose to remain in denial of a reality they cannot confront.

Denial

Denial is an incredibly powerful tool that the brain uses to avoid a reality that is too painful, scary, or overwhelming. We all look to it to protect our psyche.[1] Without knowing it, you may have experienced denial countless times in your life. You deny that when you leave the house ten minutes late, you are sure to be ten minutes late for work. You deny that your jeans fit differently since you started eating more and exercising less. You deny that your partner's words hurt your feelings because it is easier to let it go and keep the peace. You deny that your behavior contributed to an argument, that a friendship has changed, or that your dog is getting older. You deny that you are getting older. Denial is at the root of all sorts of messages we tell ourselves and all our attempts at escapism. It's sometimes momentary and other times longer; it's sometimes harmless, other times damaging. It is not always unhealthy; sometimes, denial is necessary for our well-being. When a high school classmate died during our senior year of college, a friend of mine said at the funeral: "I still expect him to call me. I still don't believe in the morning that I won't hear from him all day." My friend was there at the funeral, expressing sadness and grief and clearly accepting reality. Still, he felt a pang of denial every day. A part of him was attempting to soften the pain by fantasizing that that reality wasn't true.

Long after a big loss, even as time has passed and we have advanced far into the grieving process, we may still fall back on denial temporarily to self-soothe. To escape and "forget about life for a while," we spend nights out after work, read trashy romance novels, play role-playing games, or go on vacation.[2] Denial in itself is a necessary strategy to maintain our well-being and avoid overwhelm. As it turns out, our brains do have a pretty good grasp on what it takes to keep us alive and functioning, falling back on the fantasy game that is denial as needed. Denial, or at least escapism as a tactic, is always in motion, quietly or not so quietly, somewhere in our minds in daily life. If it weren't, the world would likely feel way too sharp, too painful.

Even those with an active understanding of and concern for climate change may sometimes use escapism to avoid thinking about it. The healthiest climate activists I know escape their work as needed, acknowledging that they just can't sit in the gravity of it *all* the time. They take weekends away to recharge; they indulge in "unsustainable" choices. They give their psyche a break from the constant onslaught of anxieties they normally endure. Most days, they choose sustainability over convenience and hard work over blissful ignorance. Other days, they tune out. I see these brief periods of escapism—making room to breathe and reset— as productive and necessary to prevent burnout from staying too serious and focused over an extended period of time. By contrast, continued denial can be extremely problematic. It is shockingly easy to deny reality; we do it frequently. Climate change threatens the very existence of our species, everything we know, and the planet we rely on. No wonder so many people are in denial. To accept that fact is to acknowledge that we are facing the biggest collective crisis imaginable. It's terrifying, and for many, it's too much.

Sometimes, we respond to bad news with, "That can't be," and we search for other perspectives that disprove it. This is not to be confused with critical thinking. I'm not saying that we shouldn't be collecting all the information we can, that we shouldn't critique and question anything that seems off base or suspect. But being skeptical because we don't have enough information is not the same as discounting reality because a lie serves us better. Denial can lead to circular arguments, while critical thinking helps us stay open to learning and changing our minds. They are difficult to differentiate if we are the ones in denial.

The biggest problem with the refusal of some to acknowledge climate change is obviously the damage to sustainability efforts. These people are finding faulty evidence to support their belief and spreading confusing misinformation, which only worsens our prognosis and delays opportunities for mitigation and healing. It is indeed frustrating to witness anyone, but especially a loved one, actively deny climate change. But while it may not look like it, people in denial—the first stage of grief—need compassion more than lectures and arguments. Of course, some may be prompted by their denial to resort to rhetoric that sounds completely believable even if it is untrue. Also, it can be argued that responses to climate change have included alarmist and overly dramatic rhetoric that doesn't help people accept it.

Generally, people who deny climate change have one of two motivations. People who stand to gain power or money from denying the truth may knowingly do so. Countless communication leaks from the fossil fuel and factory farming industries point to corporations having known about the environmental damage they cause for years. Rather than be transparent and improve sustainability standards, they have gone to great lengths to hide this information from the public and continue portraying their businesses as beneficial to humanity. Many individuals fall prey to these corporations' deceptive marketing and to misinformation disguised as healthy skepticism and "balanced" research, all of which offer an out from stark reality. They choose to listen to this messaging because it feels better. It is not as scary, it requires less work, and it allows them to feel vindicated and safe, not having to bear any obligation to the world around them. This is why so many people deny climate change, against mounting science and firsthand experiences, and basic common sense. When we frame "climate denial" in this way, it is easier to empathize with people in that phase. Denial is masking emotions we are not yet equipped to experience for the sake of self-preservation, like a band-aid our brains put on to protect us from ourselves, and all the while our subconscious is preparing to rip it off to unearth what is below: an understanding of a painful reality.

Despite any potential usefulness, denial as a defense mechanism can be destructive when it comes to the climate crisis.[3] I think that we have gotten to this point not because the problem is unsolvable but because of denial: so many people in the world are not ready to face the current situation because they do not feel empowered to solve it or responsible for solving it, even including those who are privileged enough to have the power to contribute to solutions. Many white, middle- to upper-class, educated people fall into this category, who understand what's going on and have the support and financial means to do something about it but do not want to jeopardize their lifestyles or sources of income. Until we move past denying reality because we fear the truth, we cannot contribute to solving the problem. This is true for every problem. Solutions come from only facts.

Anger

As reality seeps through the cracks of denial, the brain's next defense is anger. In this context, anger is but a secondary emotion, which coats something deeper. Anger appears after denial stops working or falls away as we feel safe enough to face the truth's painful repercussions. Anger is an emotion we know well because we regularly see it in ourselves and in others, and we use it often to hide vulnerability, to show confidence, and to feel stronger. For many people, it is the first emotion to surface. Unlike other negative emotions, anger feels like a shield rather than an open wound. As even happy emotions can create vulnerability and joy can be short-lived, anger provides protection.

When we are going through grief, anger helps us begin the process of letting emotions out. It feels good to be angry because now, at least *some* emotion is no longer trapped inside, even though fear, despair, worry, loneliness, or pain continues to hide behind that anger. The same can be said for frustration. We express frustration or anger when what we really feel leaves us emotionally exposed. Allow yourself all the time you need to feel anger. Anger is a necessary stage in our healing process; the more we feel it, the more it gives way to the feelings underneath and the readier we are to face them.

As much as it is a relief to release anger, be careful, as anger has plenty of risks. If we aren't careful and project our anger onto somebody else, we can cause irreparable relationship damage. Our anger can cause others trauma, and it can prevent our brains from exercising productive, compassionate communication. It is important for us to move through tese kinds of feelings with conscientiousness, to be able to express ourselves in a safe space with trusted people who understand us and can hold our anger with us. With an issue like climate change, displaced anger can be detrimental to our relationships and communities and ultimately make it much more difficult for us to come together to find collective solutions.

Think of a time somebody displaced their anger onto you when you had no control over a situation. Maybe you deal with the public at your job and were blamed for a customer's problem, or maybe your child took their frustration over something that happened at school out on you. On the other hand, your loved ones may often be the ones to deal with your frustration when you get home from work in a bad mood and are easily set off by clutter or noise around the house. It is understandable—though unfair—that anger often comes out sideways. Anger during the grieving process is the same and is something we must be on the lookout for lest we incur more damage to ourselves and others in times when our emotional resources are strained. Like denial, anger is not a sustainable feeling. We cannot healthfully maintain the stress hormones that are triggered when we are angry, and the relationships that help preserve our sense of safety and connection cannot thrive in the presence of anger. Whenever we feel anger, it is particularly important that our feelings are not used against others. Anger can easily lead to additional hurt and arguments, even abuse. While anger can be appropriate, angry outbursts unfairly and disproportionately aimed at others are unhealthy.

When Denial Meets Anger

Sometimes, anger points us to injustices happening to us or in the world. It tells us what really matters and what needs to change, and in expressing our anger, we help others see the same reality. Other times, the anger we feel during grieving can easily be misplaced or projected onto something that doesn't solve our problem. We may feel angry that a town didn't put up railroad crossing lights that could have prevented our loved one's accident. We may feel angry that a neighbor clear-cuts their yard when they should know about the environmental impact of clearcutting and make different choices. In some instances, our anger can be righteous and a cause for action, but that action should be taken with care.

At a conference, after my presentation on grief and anger in the context of social justice work, an attendee found me to argue the merits of anger as a necessary communication tool. He reasoned that it wakes people up to the seriousness of a problem and that we have a right to justified anger. Anger certainly gets attention. It certainly feels intense and stirs up strong emotions. Righteous anger has strengthened solidarity and camaraderie, and not to mention begotten some great songs. But often, it inspires agreement only from people who already agree. In everybody else, it stirs up fear and triggers grief that begins with (you know it!) denial. As a strategy for changing minds, anger is rarely, if ever, effective. Consider what has changed your mind in the past. Would you respond better to people yelling at you in the street, or to a trusted person having a compassionate and logical discussion with you? Shame and blame do not produce allies.

We should take notice of anger as an indicator of our inner world so that we realize what's important to us, whether we're hurting or feeling vulnerable or unsafe. But as a communication tool, anger is ineffective. By nature, our anger is hard to control or predict, it triggers a fight-or-flight response in others, and it sends them into grief via their own anger or denial. Anger-induced trauma, often from childhood, plagues many people in our society. To unknowingly trigger deep wounds and fears with our anger is no way to have a discussion or encourage change and learning.

Rarely is conflict caused by the contradiction between two equally understood facts, or two sets of equally valid concerns—although this certainly can happen, as problem solving involves managing many unknowns. Disagreement may not even result from a well-intentioned misunderstanding. Most of the time, disagreements, from relational conflict between individuals to border disputes between nations, happen because one side does not want to accept a reality, and the other feels anger over that denial. When somebody who is in deep grief and anger about climate change meets somebody in deep denial, conflict will likely arise. This is when it is absolutely critical to remember that expressing anger toward those in denial is unhealthy for everyone and ineffective at changing minds, as well as an inefficient use of time.

Most of us believe what we believe about climate science not because we have done the research, gathered the evidence, and exercised critical thinking skills, but because people around us have influenced our values and beliefs, and we have found confirmation for what we think is the truth. Denial can involve many layers, from the basic pieces of misinformation that support it to the fear that if climate change were true, the world would forever be changed. If we approach these conversations with anger, blame shifting, or emotional appeals, we risk widening the divide. For both parties' emotional safety and intellectual grounding, it is important to speak carefully, clearly, and gently. Pointing out anger or denial in another person will likely trigger alienation and defensiveness. Remember why you value the relationship and work together with the person to step toward healthy vulnerability.

Let us suppose that everybody we meet is experiencing some phase (or multiple phases) of grief. When you sense that you are about to argue about climate change, reflect on the root cause of the argument. Consider how often arguments are really about one or both sides struggling to accept the truth, not wanting to experience that reality. Anytime anger bubbles up, it is hiding a deeper pain we do not want to show. When a parent reacts with anger to a child's illness or a spouse's emotional or physical absence, underneath that anger is a fear of loss or abandonment. Likewise, underneath road rage is a fear of getting hurt or anxiety about being late for work. Anger is always blocking out an experience of vulnerability. While scary, vulnerability is almost always the right path for us to take in our relationships with others.

Bargaining

The most relieving moment in an argument is when one person takes a deep breath, puts their anger aside, and responds calmly and slowly; they're deescalating the conflict, opening the doors to mutual understanding and relationship repair. In this moment, both people have an opportunity to acknowledge that the anger wasn't helping and that something deeper is the real source of the conflict, that their connection is more important than winning the argument. We now have an opportunity to bargain with each other, to make it right. In grief, we wish for that same ability to resolve the conflict of what we have lost. At some point in our grief, our brains realize that anger does not ease our pain or change our reality. Just like yelling at the TV does not change the outcome of a game, staying angry about a loss will not take that loss away. This is when the bargaining phase of our grieving process begins.

Bargaining is about trying to compromise with the truth, and it is usually mixed with guilt and remorse we wish to escape. We may replay a past scenario and imagine we did what we now know we should have done, as we feel a sense of control in this subconscious fantasy. In an argument, bargaining may save the relationship. We figure, *I will back down and apologize, and hopefully they will too, and we can move on.* Unfortunately, with a loss, we do not have that second chance. Whatever apology we may feel compelled to share, even if what happened isn't our fault, can't change the result.

What if "if only" fantasies run through your mind in times of loss? Indeed, it may seem like putting yourself through emotional torture to think about how differently things would have turned out if only you had driven a different route and avoided that unforeseeable accident. If only your father hadn't smoked his whole life, if only you had been able to help him quit. If only you had just said something sooner. These "if only" fantasies are our brains' way of taking a brief respite from reality. Just like all the other stages of grief, bargaining comes and goes as needed, intertwining with other stages. With the death of a loved one, bargaining often moves from replaying the past to thinking about the future. We may bargain to see them in the afterlife. Indeed, some burial traditions are representative of this bargaining—to be reunited with the deceased, or to ensure their safe passage or good afterlife experience. Bargaining helps us cling to some sense of control.

That the world can be randomly cruel and unjust sometimes feels like too harsh a truth to accept. An unpredictable and uncontrollable world is hard to live in. If we maintain some sense of control over a situation, we can prevent it from ever happening again. *Lesson learned*, our brains say, *next time we can stop this!* Some part of us believes we get a second chance. Well, as you know, just like denial and anger, bargaining comes with a heavy cost: it masks the truth. It's a band-aid, which must at some point be ripped off to keep a wound from festering. Eventually, with grief, we settle into the understanding that we do not have control over the situation, and bargaining subsides as we stop secretly hoping for a redo.

I think with climate grief, bargaining can serve an exciting purpose. As long as we are alive on this planet, we have a chance to improve it. If we can imagine a plausible "if only," we can work to make the changes we want to see. Not all is lost yet. Finding the balance between accepting what has happened, accepting what is happening, and accepting responsibility for what could happen next is difficult but empowering. What if we all start bargaining for the planet? What if we all start using our imaginations to change the future? We can do that, and that is the most beautiful aspect of this stage of climate grief. Bargaining begs for control, and with climate grief, we still have some control to find.

Sadness

"I have to not harden my heart, because I want to stay open to feel things. So when I hurt, I hurt all over. And when I cry, I cry real hard. And when I'm mad, I'm mad all over. I'm just a person; I like to experience whatever the feeling is and whatever I'm going through."—**Dolly Parton** (singer, advocate of compassion and love)

Deep despair may be marked by moments of inconsolable sobbing, a visceral emptiness, or loss of appetite or sleep. While everybody feels sadness in different ways, one thing is for sure: it can feel all-consuming and inescapable. We feel sadness deep in our bones. We feel seemingly unshakeable despair, like a hole we cannot escape. Kübler-Ross compares navigating this stage of grief to sailing through the interior of a hurricane, with the looming fear of never finding the way out.[4] When we feel sadness, as horrible as it is, we are at a point where our brains are ready to incorporate reality. We are ready to know all of the truth; we have given up our struggle for control.

It certainly sucks to feel sad, but one is brave for acknowledging and sharing their sadness in whichever way feels safe and helpful. Everybody feels sadness at some point; if we don't, we aren't truly coping with anything. I admire and easily open up to people who express sadness. Sadness is easier for people to trust than denial, anger, or bargaining because it is more fully transparent and honest. A person who expresses sadness is somebody who not only is wide open to the reality of the situation but also presents themselves authentically to the world.

Unfortunately, while there is no shame in sadness, we live in a culture that despises expressions of vulnerability, from sadness to mental illnesses like depression and anxiety. When we experience sadness, we are up against society's poor relationship with it and our own fear of it. It is important to remember that depression, as part of the grieving process, is an appropriate and justified response to a very real tragedy or loss. To deny this feeling is to deny reality and to take away from the value of what we are grieving. We do ourselves a grave disservice in denying feelings of sadness, anxiety, and despair. Allowing ourselves to feel these emotions deeply and honestly helps us move through the process rather than getting stuck.

Sadness during the grieving process can be so profound that it is no wonder our brains work so hard to prepare us for the intensity and pain of it. Grief-induced depression can feel unending, bottomless, all-pervading. People have described this phase to me as completely debilitating, crushing, and seemingly impossible to overcome. Indeed, it is sometimes impossible to overcome, and we become trapped in the illness of depression.

Depression as a mental illness and depression as a stage of grief are different issues but share similar feelings and symptoms. It is never inappropriate to feel depression or anxiety. The problem with depression (and the point at which it becomes a mental illness) is that it can become truly debilitating and inhibit daily function. When sadness impacts our personal, family, and work life and robs us of full experiences for long enough, we need help getting out of it.

About one in five adults in the United States experience clinical depression or anxiety at some point in life, often stemming from an environmental trigger such as loss or disease. Thus, when we're suffering from these feelings, it is helpful to remember we are not alone. Not only that, when we experience the same trauma and loss, such as from climate change, we can find meaningful ways to move through feelings of sadness and despair together. We can draw support from others when we need it, and conversely find meaning and purpose in providing support when we are able. Doing so helps us be more honest with ourselves about how we feel. It also helps us be more vulnerable with others and develop deeper relationships that are built on a foundation of honesty and mutual support. We can find solace in knowing that our emotional reactions are normal, that others know how we feel, and that we can learn by witnessing the variety of ways in which people move through grief.

When sadness persists, find coping strategies that work for you. The hardest part is finding the energy to do anything, but at this point, it is imperative that you put in the effort to set up and attend therapy sessions, to join meetup groups, to build a structure of support around you. Use tools that have worked in the past. Tell your friends about your grief, surround yourself with books on the topic, start a new workout routine, or add healthy foods to your diet. Explore tactile stimulation by noticing sensations in the shower, listening to music, or eating more slowly. Intentionally manage sadness, acknowledge when you are using escapism, and notice how your sadness changes over time. Get to know it rather than be afraid to face it.

I do often feel deep sadness about the state of the world. Sometimes, my feelings of depression about climate change or other justice issues can last for days, even weeks before I move into a phase of better productivity. Sometimes, I have moments of sadness and am able to quickly return to joy and contentment. Other times, I begin to crave ways to escape. When I am the saddest, I enter a phase of lethargy and anxiety that can lead to burnout, sleepless nights, and long discussions with friends and family about the most painful aspects of the world.

Nonetheless, these phases also eventually help me feel motivated to get to work. I know what I worry about is important. Counteracting hopeless narratives with visions of a better future is a productive strategy to alleviate sadness and simultaneously to motivate, inspire, and spark new solutions. The only way for us to collectively begin to feel better is to make the world better. It fills me with a sense of purpose, knowing I am working on something so important. In fact, when I am struggling with depression, I do often engage in future bargaining, or hopeful meditation. I think about twenty years from now, when we will have progressed, actively improving our climate with tools and strategies unimaginable to us today, and I will have moved on to a second career. That is when I will write romance memoirs and finally learn to play the guitar.

Acceptance

Acceptance means to acknowledge the truth in its entirety, without attempting to change it by reverting to an irretrievable past, and to once again invite in neutral or positive emotions. Climate change is like any other source of grief in that we experience mourning as we settle back into daily life, knowing it will never be the same. But since climate change is so all-encompassing, we cannot easily recreate a sense of belonging or our livelihood, and we cannot rehome ourselves to escape from ongoing trauma. A victim of a burned-down home would not simply continue to live in the ashes, yet that is exactly what it feels like to grieve a dying planet.

Many have shared with me that they feel a sense of homelessness living on Earth; they are aching for what was. There is nothing bigger, better, newer, cleaner, or in a different location with which we can replace what we lost. So how do we go about accepting climate change, as all-consuming as it is? Ultimately, acceptance demands that we sit among the rubble of our burned-down home, looking for what is salvageable and rebuilding from the ashes.

The fifth stage of the grieving process enables us to realign our emotional state with the new reality of our world. It is when we fully integrate how we feel with the changes around us, when we actively reorganize our daily lives to reflect the new normal. Acceptance is an often-misunderstood stage in the grieving process as acceptance has a connotation of consent. Acceptance does not mean deciding to be okay with the situation at hand. It means simply (though maybe not so easily) acknowledging the situation as is and continuing to live in a way that reflects this. When I hear acceptance in clients' voices, it sounds like they're calmly retelling their stories. Denial and anger create a pushing or aggressive tone of voice, while sadness makes one's voice waver as they fight back emotion. Acceptance is a resolve to wholly function again.

The closer we were to a person who has passed or the more involved we were in a situation that has changed, the harder acceptance can be. With climate grief, the more we identify with a particular ecosystem that we are in danger of losing, or the more our personal lives are impacted by climate change, the trickier it is to come to terms with what is happening. It can be particularly frustrating to see that others seem not to care.

We may wish to feel the world mourn with us. It may feel like being betrayed or being left behind when others seem to have moved on or not to have noticed in the first place while we're still consumed by grief. Climate change invokes a unique grief, along with a shared responsibility to respond. Those of us who recognize it as a global threat can feel extremely frustrated, disheartened, hurt, and confused by those who don't treat their relationship with the planet with the same reverence. When an ecosystem we treasure is dying, when our homeland is ravaged by increasingly common forest fires, when our city is threatened by rising sea levels, this is not a time for mere sympathy. We want others to appreciate that this is so much more. Others' lack of acceptance can even impede our own ability to heal and readjust.

I have had an easier time accepting climate change whenever I surrounded myself with like-minded people when I was in need of comfort, laughter, transparency, or a space to feel my anger and frustration. While I of course maintain relationships with others who are not as deeply embedded in the realities of climate change, there is a certain depth of connection that I more easily achieve with those who share this fundamental understanding of the planet's crisis. It is okay to feel this way and to seek out relationships that offer this kind of connection that grounds you to keep fighting, learning, and trying. It is also okay to take some emotional space from people who do not share your grief. Yet, while those relationships may require more boundaries, when possible, maintain positive connections.

With acceptance of reality, feelings of anger, despair, and denial recede enough to make room for more compassion. You have the capacity to love the whole world. You can love the people with whom you do not agree. You can lead by example and maintain control over your thoughts, words, and actions in order to consistently enact the reality you want to see. You can reintegrate into a world filled with loss and love it as you witness whatever comes. We can do so much more through extending compassion than through clinging to old beliefs, shaming others, or getting lost in despair.

One of Martin Luther King Jr.'s most powerful statements comes from a sermon he gave in 1967: "Power at its best is love implementing the demands of justice, and justice at its best is power correcting everything that stands against love." For all I have been through, all the arguments I have engaged in, all the people I have met around the globe, each with completely unique opinions, I've found that leading with love is the only strategy that can always be justified. It is simple; it is not always easy, but if this is our goal from the start, we can get better with practice.

Meaning Making

"Action isn't a burden to be hoisted up and lugged around on our shoulders. It is something we are. The work we have to do can be seen as a kind of coming alive. More than some moral imperative, it's an awakening to our true nature, a releasing of our gifts."—**Joanna Macy** (environmental activist, scholar, pioneer of deep ecology)

As we integrate our grief into our new daily lives, we begin to feel whole again. We now have an opportunity to turn our loss into a profound experience, to celebrate memories and gifts more than the loss itself. From there, we may allow the loss to change us in ways that redirect our lives for a greater good. This is what the newly identified sixth stage of grief is all about. This stage—meaning making—ushers us into endless possibilities, empowering us to give our impassioned hearts a purpose and find ways to embody the changes we want to see.

After Kübler-Ross's death in 2004, her student David Kessler continued building and has since added to the body of research on grief. After experiencing the loss of his twenty-one-year-old son, Kessler coined the term *meaning making* to define and describe the final stage of grief, wherein we take our grief and make something of it. As he said: "Meaning comes through finding a way to sustain your love for the person after their death while you're moving forward with your life. Loss is simply what happens to you in life. Meaning is what *you* make happen."[5] This is exemplified by organizations like Mothers Against Drunk Driving, by survivors who in turn sponsor those in a similar situation or seek a mission-driven career to fix a bigger problem. In each case, restoration through helping others and solving collective problems helps us honor the past.

A generation before Kessler and Kübler-Ross, Victor Frankl had established the importance of meaning making in his book *Man's Search for Meaning*. A psychologist who survived the Holocaust, Frankl identified a sustained sense of purpose as a key survival tactic in concentration camps. Those who survived were the ones who kept alive a desire for meaning and a belief that even in the worst situation, purpose could be salvaged or created, whereas people who lost their sense of meaning or purpose were less likely to make it. Rather than just hoping the struggle would end, focusing on a bigger purpose helped survivors get through days that brought others despair, such as personal milestones and holidays.

If we can make meaning out of climate grief, we can occupy ourselves with tasks that create positive change and a sense of hope. While we may question the effectiveness of our individual efforts, we need only look at Holocaust survivors, among many others, who did what they felt was right or healthiest in the moment and somehow created a remarkable change in the end. At any rate, what we know is that giving up is absolutely unhelpful. As some of my favorite mentors have said, the only universal rule is just "to not do nothing."

Consider the passion and dedication of the students in Parkland, Florida, who survived a school shooting and now work to change federal gun laws. Or the boldness and conviction of Greta Thunberg, who has decided to fight back against climate change by appealing to politicians and inspiring others to get involved. How about your own experience with loss and trauma—what changes did you incorporate to move toward a healthier or more informed way of living? Maybe you have helped others going through the same problem, or maybe you have adjusted your beliefs and stances. When we learn from what happened and let it inform our future, we are creating meaning from that experience.

I learned to grieve not from climate change but from a childhood friend's passing. I grew up with three other girls, who had become my best friends partly by choice and partly by circumstance, as we were the only girls in our grade all the way from kindergarten to sixth grade in our tiny elementary school. Of the four of us, Teddi was the assertive one. She was the leader of our pack, with a voice and determination that both far outpunched her tiny stature. She wanted to be the president of the United States someday, and nobody would have been surprised had she grown up to accomplish it. In seventh grade, she was killed by her father in a murder-suicide that shook our small community. Her death left me in a tailspin of grief and shock for weeks and months to come. For the next two decades, I did a lot of soul searching, therapy, spiritual exploration, reading, and anything else that might help me make sense of what had happened. I couldn't justify how someone I'd seen as a father figure could turn into the monster that killed my friend. The loss forced me to challenge the basic human psychological tendency toward binary thinking. Either father figures could not be trusted or Teddi had deserved it, or something else was true. It challenged my religious belief that everything happened for a reason. Finally, it led me to examine what difference I could or should try to make with my life.

Eventually, I started a project to help victims of domestic abuse. There was a need for safe housing that allowed animals, and this gap proved to be one of the biggest reasons why victims did not leave dangerous situations, often leading to tragic outcomes. I knew that pets needed to be included in crisis response. As I worked on the logistics of the project and saw the positive responses from community members, I realized I was answering a real need. Completing the project lifted some of the invisible weight I'd been carrying with me for the two decades after Teddi's death. I still felt the pain of loss; I still had moments of overwhelming grief, anger, and sadness; but creating a meaningful way to help others was therapeutic. The project encapsulated my grief. I could not bring Teddi back, nor could I, in any real way, intellectualize, minimize, or escape the trauma of that experience. I could create something that would grow from the ashes. I could keep her legacy alive, not by rewriting her ending but by adding a chapter.

Making meaning out of an experience—any experience—is what gives the experience its value. We value our environment; therefore, we find deep meaning and grief in our concern for it. At this point, we can choose to focus on meaning making to define our relationship with climate change. Doing so may not immediately or effectively influence the overall reality of climate change: making meaning out of any loss does not change the fact of that loss. But we have to let go of our desire to control or fully annihilate our suffering, which is inherent in the experience of being human, of being a sentient animal on Earth. In coping with climate grief, we won't get to a point where we no longer grieve. Rather, it is a regular practice that enables us to chip away at the sharpness of our pain. Sometimes, the best we can do is to respond with created meaning and hope because it's the right thing to do, even if it may not make a difference. After all, what if it does?

One may have a hard time imagining what meaning making looks like unless one has successfully done it before. We find meaning in small losses too, many times throughout our lives. Consider a time when you may have missed a big meeting, or gotten caught cheating on a test, or had your car broken into. Small lessons learned from more benign experiences help us remember to try our best and prepare ourselves—to be kinder, to take better care of our belongings, to feel empathy for others, or to stop overvaluing belongings we don't even need. Finding meaning is taking away a lesson or advocating for what we love. With respect to climate change, meaning making can look like focusing on local species and ecosystems on which we do have direct influence, or recording environmental losses as they happen via photography or writing. It is using our grief to propel action, so that others can sense the urgency and importance of the problem.

The Purpose of Grief

The stage of meaning making is the most helpful to us as we try to integrate our pain so as to live more healthfully and wholeheartedly, to practice better self-care in spite of whatever is going on in the world. If we can develop the strength, resilience, and resolve required to find meaning in our suffering, we can then create transformative change not just for ourselves but for the planet. Working through the grieving process frees you from getting stuck in denial, anger, or despair that, when left unprocessed, can poison your outlook or even your entire personality.

As you navigate the various stages of grief, try to appreciate the purpose behind each stage and let the experience remind you of the importance of your loss. Grief should not be shame-inducing but bittersweet. The more you practice paying attention to grief, the better you get at working with it, recognizing what you need out of it, and even managing it. To me, grief sometimes feels like a lucid dream in which I can recognize that I am grieving. I know I need to go along with it. I know I shouldn't fight it, and I feel the need to stay in it, to stay with it. I come out the other side with a stronger connection to my inner voice, to my emotions. I come out stronger and more aware.

It is only through processing grief that we can build back real strength and resilience, and it's a long, intentional, deliberate practice that will get us there. If grief processing were easy, we would have far fewer poets and artists, songs and paintings . . . and pubs. The struggle is the point. What we are losing due to climate change is important to us and thus captures our attention. The first meaning that can be generated from grief, I find, is an appreciation for the value of what has been lost. To notice our hurt is to pay homage to its source. How insensitive and ungrateful would we be to arrive at a loved one's funeral and have no emotions to offer?

Processing grief results in solving the right problems. When we misidentify the source of our pain, our attempts to cope won't lead to relief. By contrast, correctly identifying the source of our pain frees us to really heal. Once we acknowledge our climate grief and find ways to cope with it, we can become better engaged in the process of fighting climate change.

Collectively, we created a mess. We will keep making it worse until we slow down and act with compassion for ourselves and others. Let's not accept our current reality as the apex of our evolution. Even when climate-related disagreements happen, don't equate another's current opinions or choices with their core identity. We are all learning and growing—and changing as a result. Imagine the peace we can find for ourselves, the welcoming space we can make for each other, and the sustainable and equitable world we can create for all beings.

3
TOOLS FOR RESILIENCE AND WELL-BEING

"To be fully alive, fully human, and completely awake is to be continually thrown out of the nest."—**Pema Chödrön**
(Tibetan Buddhist nun, teacher)

The secret to a healthy, happy life is figuring out how to live well in spite of and within a heavy and uncertain world. The uncertainties don't go away, and ignoring them won't produce health or real contentment. Well-being comes by balancing stressors with sources of joy, inner turmoil with a core sense of peace. Resilience is the ability to find this balance during difficult times—even as the urgency and existential stress of climate change hang over our heads—and to withstand and successfully adapt to life's challenges. Resilience and well-being can be cultivated and further strengthened through intentional practice.

The Harvard Study of Adult Development, which spanned nearly eighty years, found that the factor that had the biggest influence on both happiness and longevity was having healthy relationships and community.[1] Consider people you know who seem happy and healthy throughout their whole lives. The happiest people I know are those who focus on giving, learning, and growing in community. They aren't necessarily the wealthiest or the most driven. Rather than financial wealth, what stands out is their willingness to acknowledge their problems with honesty (they are not afraid to show vulnerability) and to care deeply about others and the planet. To me, these people present to the outside world an aura of resilience; strength and confidence emanate from their commitment to do good. Brené Brown captures this essence in her description of wholehearted living, which, to paraphrase, is a sense of belonging and completeness achieved through living with compassion and in community.[2] Across all the different ways to think about happiness, well-being, and wholeheartedness, the dominant theme is not a life without problems but a life filled with active and hopeful problem solving.

It may seem impossible to adequately help both ourselves and the planet, to focus on our own well-being while still putting our community first. On the contrary, it's impossible not to do both, as individual well-being and collective well-being are intertwined. When collaborating with other wholehearted and innovative people, we feel empowered, experience a shared sense of belonging, and often achieve success. Wholehearted community living is a value that conflicts with capitalism, however, so we have to navigate questions of whom we can rely on, when to protect ourselves, and where to compromise. When injustices are justified, even exacerbated, by societal norms, such as when society directs our focus toward personal finance away from systemic causes of inequality, thus widening the gap between the rich and the poor, well-being for much of the community has been neglected from the start. Victims of exploitation endure circumstances that can make living well and resiliently especially difficult. When I reflect on what it means to pursue health and happiness, it is always with heavy acknowledgement that I am doing so thanks to privileges that so many people around the world do not currently have.

For those of us lucky enough to have been born with basic opportunities and rights, how should we be building community, resilience, and well-being? If humans are born with the capacity to take good or bad actions, to build happiness or misery, to support justice or evil, what are the levers that determine our choices? To do well as a human is to maintain a healthy reverence for everyone and everything, from one's very own body to the entire world, which means one's drive for self-preservation must align with the preservation of one's community. Life is a series of constant lessons in how to live well with others. The trick is to learn how to do this within the current socio-economic and political systems without losing our grounding in community.

Living well means working to take care of ourselves, physically and mentally, and to adjust as we learn to live more sustainably, build community, and create change where it's needed. Living well means understanding that we are all connected within a big system (bigger than any human-created system) and that anything we contribute to this system will affect all of us. Healthy, balanced, compassionate community living is plausible even in this time of climate crisis, giving us hope for sustainable living long into the future. When I think about what living well looks like, a few of my mentors come to mind, as does a retired couple I know that hasn't slowed much at all despite being in retirement, as they are building a sustainable home and traveling to volunteer a few times a year. Another couple I know has a new homesteading project going every season, has mastered composting and small-scale gardening, and plans to grow mushrooms on their property next. Yet another good friend of mine attends therapy every week as a self-care ritual. In this chapter, we will cover some of the best ways to achieve this kind of well-being.

Live the Change You Want Out Loud

And in the end
The love you take
Is equal to the love you make.
—The Beatles' song "The End"

To feel more happiness, make your choices as if the life you want to live were already here. Practice living the reality you want to see. Do you wish everybody biked to work? Only ate local and organic foods? Had a giant garden in their front yard? In whatever ways you can, make sustainable and healthy choices as opportunities arise. Focus on yourself and on living in alignment with your values and goals. In making this the starting point, I don't mean to sound flippant. Of course, I am not saying, "If you want to be happy, *just, you know, make the choice to be happy!*" This is not about toxic or fake positivity but about practicing doing what brings you joy.

Well-being and resilience are built from a daily focus on what is within your control rather than an obsession with what isn't. Don't make your daily choices based on feelings of anger and bitterness, on escapism, or on an estimation of success or failure. Make choices that reflect your personal ethics, which will enable you, through your lifestyle, to show what matters most to you. Let your value-driven life give rise to a feedback loop of positivity, no matter how small. When you do so, people around you will know who you are and what you want. Authenticity breeds positive energy, builds community, and delivers results. Cultural change may be the biggest factor in determining if, then when and how, we will mitigate climate change enough to maintain life on the planet. Cultural change only happens when people live the change they want out loud.

Start with the bigger picture and design your life such that you can live your values out loud. Be an example of what you think ethical living looks like, including practicing self-compassion and good old basic self-care. Develop habits that center your intentions around your personal coping and resilience. The tools we can use to cope with grief are as universal as the feelings of grief. The best climate grief-coping strategies I have observed are compassion, healthy communication and community, therapy, meditation and reflection, physical exercise, time with nature, time away from stressors, healthy food, and good sleep. We know these help us feel better for a variety of reasons, yet it's common to feel guilty when we pursue them. Many activists and caretakers are driven daily by a sense of responsibility to do everything possible for their cause, leaving little energy for their own needs. Driving yourself to burnout and despair is unhealthy and counterproductive. You can't find joy in burnout, so it's no wonder that we lose motivation when we push ourselves to save something or strive for a goal that isn't even a source of joy for us. This is the most compelling reason why you should prioritize yourself. You can't do the work when you are burned out or unhealthy. Self-care habits are not selfish or indulgent, but imperative. Remember, individual sustainability and ecosystem sustainability are intertwined!

I say this not as an expert on maintaining a consistent self-care routine but as an expert on the dangers of *not* prioritizing self-care. I can find plenty of ways to sidetrack myself, plenty of distractions that throw me off course from my desired routine. What I have learned is that when I am taking care of myself with my favorite self-care activities, I do feel a difference in my body.

I feel more focused and lighter, and I am more productive. I still feel grief, and I still have days when bad news about the climate can turn me into a puddle of anger and tears. Building resilience is not about losing those honest reactions but about maintaining our desire to live and to feel joy, as well as our connections to our inner selves and to others. Healthy self-care really is the secret to a resilient human, community, and planet—all parts of an interdependent system and thus, in a way, one and the same. Gone should be the perspective that doing good for others means you can't take care of your own needs, or that you have to prioritize meeting your needs over making the world better. If you're truly doing something good for yourself, the planet benefits too.

Compassion

"Love isn't a state of perfect caring. It is an active noun like struggle."—**Fred Rogers** (television host, author, advocate of compassionate living)

For so many clients and friends who have shared their struggles with me, the biggest source of climate grief isn't even the problem itself but their guilt from not doing "enough" to solve the problem. I've witnessed many lose entire days to punishing themselves through anxiety and indecision, never feeling adequate. I've watched people berate themselves for taking a vacation or needing a week away. A dear friend of mine feels so distraught about climate change that she takes part in every climate justice event and volunteer group she can. She counts bird nests and protects monarch cocoons; she signs petitions and goes to rallies. She bikes, reuses everything, and is in a constant battle with herself to do better. Still, trying to do everything leaves her feeling like she doesn't do enough, like she has no skills to contribute because she's spread too thin.

There are multiple healthy approaches my friend could take to resolve this conflict. She could focus on fewer tasks to dedicate more time and energy to each task or to build in more time for *herself*. She could even embrace what she's currently doing and decide that she *enjoys* being engaged in so many communities at once. The point is that any option is good if she can believe it's "good enough." It may not even be her chaotic schedule of myriad of responsibilities that's destroying her well-being, but her insistence that she should always be doing more. If you—like my friend—find that a lack of self-compassion is hurting your health, I invite you to go gentler on yourself. Celebrate just how much you do. What if it were actually plenty?

In the past, I myself tended to self-sabotage by obsessing over my own "shoulds," being so stressed by them that I actually accomplished less and was less effective than I could be, until I realized what the root of the problem was. One of my favorite activists talks a lot about taking time to recharge. He goes on hikes for several days at a time; he spends time during the day alone relaxing; and he exercises. Whether you are going through a phase in which you need to focus more on yourself, or you are new to activism and want to start slow, or you need to step back from a position of leadership to recharge, or you recognize and honor your waxing and waning energy levels, it is okay and your struggle is valid. The journey is long; we change and grow in ways that are more like walking through a labyrinth than running down a straight road.

Another thing we shouldn't do is sabotage *others* with our "shoulds." Just as our self-judgment is toxic to ourselves, our judgment about others is unfair and toxic to our community.

Judging others is a way to feel better about what we're doing, but it only wastes good energy and produces negative energy. Living in a sustainable community requires rooting out all toxic judgment. Inclusivity and love cannot coexist with condemnation. You are better off exploring where that judgment comes from within yourself so you can heal rather than project it. Is it jealousy, fatigue, or fear? Is there frustration when somebody else's values don't align with yours? If it is something out of your control, let it go. If you can help the other person, and they want help from you, help. It is not your job to convince people to do good in the world. Instead, offer to support and collaborate with somebody who shares your perspective or is open to hearing it. Focus on projecting love and compassion.

Communication and Community

Growing up in the Midwest, I learned the art of passive communication. The Midwestern culture I knew was built by descendants of Scandinavians, characterized by muted expression and an absence of shared emotion. Kindness and accommodation were strong values, but so much passivity meant a lack of emotional honesty. A friend of mine from New England, who married into a Minnesota family, lamented that it had taken years for her to be able to guess what her in-laws were thinking. In her family of origin, there was never any need to guess, as family members wore their excitement, their sadness, and their conflicts on their sleeves. This is not to say that a lack of emotional boundaries is better, as emotional aggressiveness has its own problems.[3] What I am suggesting is that whichever subcultures we may hail from, we all have to work toward healthy communication. People pleasing, competitiveness, and other maladaptive motivations engendered by culture or family dynamics lead to misunderstandings and limit how effective our communication can be.

Aggressive communication lacks kindness, and passive communication lacks honesty. Kind and honest communication is assertiveness. Being kind and honest requires us to be careful with our words and to be honest about our feelings even if it leaves us vulnerable. Vulnerability, honesty, and kindness build relationships and community and are needed for healthy communication. Sadly, social emotional learning (which covers emotion regulation, empathy, and relationships) isn't a big part of K-12 education, currently oriented toward protecting children's physical safety and teaching for mandated standardized testing. As adults, we teach children only what we know; to raise a generation that cares about improving communication and building community, we must intentionally break old cultural patterns.

Individual mental health is so interconnected with community and healthy communication that it should be a top priority of ours to build community wellness around mental healthcare and healthy communication. To have good emotional insight, contribute to healthy family dynamics, and be fully emotionally present in relationships, we have to prioritize mental health, and we have to prioritize communicating about mental health and grief with each other. When you are struggling, say so. When you are confused or drained, tell people. When you find something that invigorates and empowers you, celebrate it. Practice open, kind, honest communication every chance you get. Because you likely did not grow up learning healthy communication styles and patterns, there may be bad habits to unlearn as you define your goals and what constitute healthy habits. Bad habits may manifest themselves in the way we do or don't communicate, in the way we do or don't show up for others when they are trying to communicate theirs, or in our own needs and emotions. Vulnerability feels uncomfortable, not just to the person being vulnerable but also to the person with whom vulnerability is shared. Why is this? Consider what vulnerability feels like to you when you are being vulnerable with others. What were you taught growing up about expressing emotions, experiencing grief, or communicating your mental health needs? Realizing the symbiotic relationship between mental health and communication can transform you and your community.

Building a supportive community takes effort from everybody. Assuming you have a circle of people willing to be open and vulnerable, together, you can create a network of support. You may need to take the first step and put your own emotions out there. While intimidating, doing so is far better than missing out on potentially beautiful connections. If you haven't yet talked to many people about your climate grief, try; you may find that others feel similarly or can show up for you with support if you just ask. You may seek professional help if you don't feel like you have the necessary skills or like you don't have a community with the same goal as you. Either way, therapy is a big tool for communication skill development.

Therapy

Mental health therapy has the potential to change one's life. When a client is ready to do the work and can find a suitable therapist, therapy can make a profound difference in their functioning. I cannot recommend therapy enough for everybody. Having a therapist is different from talking to friends and family because therapists are trained professionals and likely strong communicators who are prepared to focus entirely on a client's needs. They know how to help a person explore emotions and set up a plan for healing and recovery. There are therapists who specialize in ecotherapy, which is therapy centered around the human–nature relationship. Ecotherapists are specially equipped to help clients experiencing climate grief.

Exploring different approaches and shopping for a well-fitting therapist are of course much easier when one has the time and financial means. Less costly options include sliding-scale fees, insurance coverage, and more affordable support group settings. Therapy does take energy, effort, and often financial resources, and it is not yet accessible to all as it should be.

It may also be difficult to find a therapist well versed in supporting somebody with climate grief, as the concept is still relatively unfamiliar to many therapists. Even then, it takes more energy than one might imagine to truly make use of the therapeutic process. However, the benefits can extend to every one of your relationships and every aspect of your day-to-day life. Books written by therapists, podcasts about mental health, and peer-developed groups such as book clubs can also be therapeutic. While finances are an unfortunate barrier for many people, by exploring community resources available to you, you may find that therapy is within reach.

Therapy can be particularly helpful if you're still honing the skills to create open communication with your community or if you lack a community with which you can openly communicate your emotional experience. If you are unsure how to build a lifestyle based on your ethics regarding the environment, an ecotherapist (or a life coach) can offer transformative support. Therapy can help with following through on goals and new habits, from creating community to establishing a meditation routine to sticking to health resolutions.

Mindfulness, Meditation, and Breathwork

The point of mindfulness, meditation, and breathwork is to redirect focus onto the body. It is easy to be distracted by everything going on outside of us, to be pulled in all directions by obligations and other people. When we lose focus on our bodies, our breathing becomes shallower when we get stressed. This can trigger our fight-or-flight response, increase our anxieties, and decrease our overall functionality. When our minds get busy, we miss out on details around us and within us. Taking the time for stillness and reflection helps us reconnect to our own feelings and to the subtle details of our daily experiences. Breathwork, meditation, and mindfulness can help us come up with insights, solve problems, and exercise creativity.

The spiritual discipline of yoga is one tool for connecting to breath, practicing meditation, and maintaining physical health. What is generically referred to as yoga usually encompasses only the exercise aspect; in fact, the tradition is much more far-reaching. Rooted in ancient Indian culture, yoga is a strategy for uniting mind and body and is often part of a spiritual practice. I have found yoga to be very helpful in increasing my ability to be mindful throughout my day, as well as my capacity for meditation and breathwork. While you should be wary of problematic appropriations of yoga practices in the Western world, it is rewarding to respectfully explore yoga and find a practice that fits your goals.

There are as many options for how to practice yoga as there are people practicing it. You don't have to make yours a long practice. Whether you commit to just five minutes of total silence, follow along to a meditation online, or join a group, you will notice changes in your body. I taught at a yoga studio where one of my fellow teachers posted mindfulness and breathwork videos online. He had a calming voice and offered simple mantras I could return to in my mind for the rest of the day as needed. When I followed his channel, my meditation practice became something I would look forward to every morning, something I could practice before even having to get out of bed. There are online meditations created specifically for those worried about climate change. You can create your own mindfulness practice in nature too. For many, reflection is tied to a spiritual or religious exercise, but it doesn't need to be. It may just be a time you use to explore open-ended questions and may even help you define your spirituality. Personally, I've always found gardening to be my preferred meditation task; while gardening, I feel a connection to something greater than myself, to what I perceive to be *holy*.

Physical Activity

Physical activity in this context isn't about fitting into a certain fitness mold or achieving a certain weight or ideal body type. I bring up physical activity because being active aids the overall functioning of the body and supports organ, muscle, tissue, and bone health. Movement can reduce stress, improve sleep, and remind you that your body is alive. This is about what exercise does for you internally and what abundant health and energy feel like in your body.

Any activity or movement is great if it leaves you feeling accomplished, content, at peace, and either tired or energized (depending on what you're looking for). Our bodies were specifically designed for motion, and we move for a myriad of good reasons. We consume energy, quantified as calories, and are meant to burn it through movement; therefore, a sedentary, indoor human body likely feels like an unnatural and discontented body. We evolved to walk, run, dance, lift things, hear and smell nature, and feel the sunshine. Our bones get stronger with some stress, and our muscles improve with stretching and flexing. Our lungs, heart, and brain all benefit from the blood flow that physical activity encourages. Give yourself the priceless gift of activity. Do whatever works for you, and make the commitment to yourself to do it consistently. Treat it like part of your job. Get the whole family involved. Your well-being depends on it, and feeling good in your body should not be sacrificed or devalued. Physical movement is important self-care.

The benefits of exercise to the mind, body, and spirit are well documented. If you struggle to find the motivation to exercise, consider the source of that barrier. Is it self-consciousness, time, money, or past experiences? Whatever is keeping you stuck, reflect on it and find a solution to the problem. If it is about time or money, incorporate small changes into your daily routine, like walking the stairs during your commute or parking farther away, or go for a walk after picking up your kids instead of succumbing right away to your devices. Get creative and pursue new solutions if what you've tried in the past hasn't worked for you. My favorite recent change in routine has been going for walks with my best friend after her work day instead of going to happy hour. Sometimes, solutions are so simple and obvious, yet we don't think of them as we get stuck in what we're used to.

In a similar vein, budgeting forced me to see a better solution to an issue in my typical day. Instead of paying for parking at the college where I teach, I found free parking off campus, exactly one third of a mile from my building. I began leaving my house ten minutes earlier each day to do the extra walk up the hill, until I realized I was actually getting to my classroom earlier. I hadn't noticed how much time I had been spending driving around looking for parking in the paid lot! A bonus was that the free parking was at a community trail entrance. At the end of my teaching day, I'd change into my running gear to run on the trail. Thus, I would have spent time in nature and gotten a great workout in by the time I got home every day, in addition to saving $125 per semester and having to sacrifice very little time. Where there is motivation, there is a strategy for a better solution. Remember that the goal is not to become an athlete or to lose weight (unless you want to). The goal is to give your body the chance to use its energy and flush out stress hormones, and to engage your brain by giving it a break from other work.

Time Away, Time in Nature

Physical activity is one way to carve out time to be in nature and to be alone; for me, my preferred spiritual practice of gardening allows me to achieve the same end. We all need breaks from our work and routine. Even extroverts need time alone to defragment their minds. There is plenty of research on the many benefits of taking a break from our work and the impossibility of ongoing productivity. The more you listen to your mind and body and follow your inner voice, the more you may find yourself craving alone time, or time in the woods, in national parks, or on the beach. Follow these cravings! They lead you to feeling more whole, more at ease, more connected to nature.

Taking a break looks different for each of us, for each phase in life, and as our surroundings change. When I finally moved to a warmer climate, I realized that I had been craving more sunshine. I was happy to find that daily time outdoors in easy weather influenced my outlook on life tremendously. I recovered from some emotional struggles I'd been having, and I became physically healthier.

Nature has a way of demanding our attention. As I write this, I am sitting on a raft floating on a small pond in my best friend's yard. A small bee has been wandering around on my foot, and I wonder if they are finding some tiny useful nutrient in the sand stuck to my skin. Maybe they are just curious about what this huge creature is. I wonder if they realize they are on another being, or if they realize they are safe with me. The distraction brings my heart rate down noticeably and gives me a rejuvenating smile. Even if we cannot change our location to surround ourselves with sunshine or wildlife, we can find or create some piece of the natural world that we need in our daily experience.

Sleep

"Sleep is the best meditation."—**Tenzin Gyatso**
(14th Dalai Lama)

Several studies published in recent years have highlighted the benefits of adequate sleep. From stress reduction to improved brain function and heart health, the list of benefits from good sleep is long. Everybody has a unique circadian rhythm and ideal sleep/wake cycle, but most adults in modern society are not getting enough sleep. Sleep deprivation can impair brain function the next day and, in the long term, increase the risk of cancers and other diseases and contribute to weight gain. Given the damage done to our bodies and brains when we do not sleep enough, it is a shame that leading a stressful, sleep-deprived life is practically a badge of honor in American culture. Imagine how much more (higher-quality) work we could get done if we prioritized sleep.

A year or two after I had finished my PhD, I still behaved like all-nighters were some sort of badge of honor and being very busy meant my work was very important. Though I didn't consciously think this, it was apparently a subconscious belief, as I packed my schedule so full that I didn't have a choice but to sacrifice sleep. At the time, I was teaching developmental psychology to undergraduate nursing students. During a lesson on sleep, I asked students to write on the board their average numbers of hours of sleep. Some were as low as four hours, a few were as high as nine hours, but most students reported sleeping five to six hours per night. As I lectured them about the importance of sleep in aiding everything from mood regulation, metabolism, skin elasticity, to brain function, it sank in that I was sleeping less than most undergraduate college students. They lived in dormitories, had constant deadlines, were just getting a handle on basic adult responsibilities, and fed gaming addictions. What in the world was I doing?! Now, a few years later, I can't even recall the work I was doing back then. I was prioritizing forgettable productivity over present and future health.

Then, I did an experiment. As I wrote this book, I noted how many hours I slept and how many pages I wrote or edited. I realized that I was far more productive with more sleep, even when I spent over two additional hours in bed. I felt like I looked better, and I could not identify any other change in my daily schedule. This helped me prove to myself that I operate better on good sleep. If you can, budget more time to sleep. If you can't, take time to create an ideal sleeping space. Invest in some melatonin pills; get black-out curtains, some fancy pillows, and the best comforter ever. Take care of your body so it can sleep the best it can, when it can. Sleeping better will help you live better.

Eat Well

Growing up in a space wild enough for me to see seasonal change opened my eyes to the planet's abundance. The Minnesota summer sun promoted incredibly fast plant growth. As a kid, I felt I could almost watch berries change colors and lettuce grow in the garden in real time. I was shocked that food could be so easily and quickly grown! Still, most of our food came from grocery stores. Wild-foraged or harvested foods were more a novelty than a staple. Pressed to maintain two incomes, the post-WWII generations have seen a drastic decrease in small-scale food production. Only recently has there been a resurgence in foraging, backyard gardening, and support for locally grown agriculture.

This back-to-nature shift is great news, as the healthiest food available to us is what's grown organically and nearby. Time and distance decrease nutritional value, especially as travel-bound fruits and vegetables are picked well before they ripen, then treated with color additives or protective waxes. Traveling food tends to come from large-scale agricultural operations that rely heavily on chemicals. The healthiest food we can find is organic food grown in fertile, healthy soil and with safe, drinkable water, then eaten close to its source. Riper and containing fewer pesticides, it's also less stressful on our bodies to digest, which is important for our longevity. This is partly why fruits, vegetables, and grains do our bodies the most good, while meat and dairy are generally more difficult to metabolize (and also much more environmentally destructive). Luckily, what is healthiest for our bodies is healthiest for our climate too.

The human body is built much like those of other herbivores, with jaws that move from side to side, molars that can grind plant matter, and a lack of large fanged teeth or claws. We have an extremely long intestinal tract that holds on to plant food long enough to absorb its complex nutrient content and process the fiber. Our long digestive tract also makes us more vulnerable to absorbing and getting sick from bacteria, which is why we have to cook meat. We are unlike omnivores and carnivores, who have much shorter intestines and can eat raw and rotting carcasses without concern. In addition, the majority of adult humans cannot naturally digest the lactose in dairy, and when we do consume animal products, we take in more saturated fat and cholesterol than our bodies can healthfully use. Cardiovascular diseases, type 2 diabetes, and certain types of cancer are all directly linked to meat-heavy diets. If you have never tried reducing your meat or dairy intake, consider doing so while increasing the variety and amount of vegetables you eat. Consider trying a vegetarian or vegan diet and note what changes occur in your body. You may notice a variety of benefits to your health, physical and emotional, from consuming foods that can be more easily prepared and digested.

I have changed my diet several times in my life, though most of the time, better health was not my primary motivation. Still, when I shifted to an entirely plant-based diet, there were a few compelling physical benefits. I noticed that my singing voice improved, as I hadn't realized that consuming milk had been creating more mucus in my throat and was even causing vocal cord damage. I also noticed that my skin seemed smoother and clearer and that my body weight stabilized without additional effort. The biggest difference, however, was in my endurance and general physical fitness. I had recently gotten into distance running and had run a few marathons. I was not a die-hard runner by any stretch of the imagination, nor did I fantasize about breaking any records. But then, break records I did.

I was creating a postdoctoral project to raise awareness about water pollution from resource-exploiting industries in the North Shore region of Lake Superior. Over the course of nine days, I ran about 300 miles through the Superior Hiking Trail in northern Minnesota (and walked plenty too). Along the way, I interviewed researchers, activists, and community leaders, all with stories to tell about the effects of mines, pipelines, and pollution on our lake. The project captured some attention from people interested in the running itself. It was a notable distance to cover in a short period of time, on a single track over difficult terrain—crossing roots, rocks, cliffs, beaches, and even swamps. I admit even I was surprised that, minus some miles on particularly rainy days and a section of the trail being closed due to a storm, I finished with a daily average of 33 miles of running.

After I finished the run, I visited the doctor; some swelling in my leg had me worried. The doctor checked me over, took some blood tests, and asked me for details about the run. I explained that I mostly didn't think about what I was eating. I ate when I was hungry, and it was mostly peanut butter or ramen at campsites in the evening. Not an ideal, balanced meal plan, I realized, but if a body hard at work had cravings, I figured I wouldn't argue. When he came back with the bloodwork, he was astonished. He had expected to see important levels out of balance, and that I'd need electrolytes, protein, and iron. He looked up from his clipboard and said: "Your bloodwork is the best I've ever seen. What were you eating before you left? You must have been taking impeccably good care of yourself."

I told him what I always explain about my diet: I eat what I feel like eating, when I feel like eating it. I make sure my everyday intake includes a variety of colors. That's about all the thought I put into it. As a vegan, I eat a lot of colors to ensure I'm not just eating processed stuff, and when most of my food is in the form of fruits, veggies, and grains, there is no need to limit myself. The doctor responded to my actual concern about my leg: "Your swelling is just water retention around your joints, since joints don't enjoy that much pounding for so many miles. By tomorrow night, you'll be peeing a lot, and then the swelling should be gone. And I need to seriously consider changing my diet." I thanked him for the reassurance and went home to bed. He was right; by the next day, I was playing sand volleyball and moving around like the run hadn't happened.

That run was one of many that I did without a traditional training or meal plan. I moved my body a lot, doing whatever fun activity I could find, and continued to eat what my body seemed to want. For every trail race, every long day of volleyball or tennis or rollerblading, I felt strong and well-conditioned. This is not to say a plant-based diet is a miracle drug that will cure everything and make life easier in every way for every person. My point is more that it is very possible, and actually easier for many, to thrive on a plant-based diet. I generally feel less fatigue, brain fog, and depression than I remember feeling when I still consumed dairy. But maybe it isn't all diet. These improvements could also have to do with my living in alignment with my values of sustainability, compassion, and nonviolence, which was my intention in going plant-based in the first place. Maybe there are some inflammatory foods that accompany non-vegan diets that I am now avoiding by default. Whatever the causes, the result is a happier me. It's easy for me to maintain this lifestyle because it feels really good.

Whatever eating well means in your life, it's a part of self-care that is worthy of consideration and that will promote well-being and resilience. Our food is the gas we put into the tank. If it is highly processed, filled with additives we do not need and have not evolved to process, it will negatively affect how our bodies operate. The typical American diet is not the healthiest option for us or for the planet, and there is a lot about our food system and individual diets we can change to promote healthier living.

Create Your Plan

"Write it down to make it happen."—**Marian Lansky** (artist)

Take time to reflect on how you grieve and how you cope. Consider the following questions. Personally, I would take out some paper and write until I felt like I knew my own grief better. I revisit these questions every year or whenever I feel stuck in my grief and unsure how to feel better. Once, I even created a spreadsheet to track how my grief experiences compared with each other and to see how my grieving process evolved over time. I hope this exercise helps you reflect on your experience and make a plan for coping as much as it has helped me.

- When throughout your life have you felt grief?
- Each time you have been in grief, what helped you feel better?
- What has helped you move through grief the most?
- When have you felt your healthiest—physically, mentally, emotionally, and socially? What were your daily habits?
- When do you feel climate grief most strongly?
- Do you have unhealthy or unhelpful habits that are coping strategies? How can you reduce your dependence

on them or reframe their role in your life (if you still want to keep them at all)?

- What coping strategies would you like to try, add, or continue?
  - Do you currently or could you communicate your concerns in a creative way (through music, writing, etc.)?
  - Who is in your climate grief community? Who do you or can you talk to about climate grief? Can you create a schedule or intention to reach out to them?
  - How can you create a safe place for others to grieve or to learn with you?
  - Would you like to create a new menu by taking miles, animals, plastic packaging, or industrial agriculture off your plate?
  - Do you have, or would you like to create, a mindfulness practice?
  - How can you continue to tend to your own emotional growth?
- When you think about a sustainable future, what does the world look like in your mind?
  - What can you do, big or small, to bring any part of that world to reality now?

Lead with Love

"A purpose of human life, no matter who is controlling it, is to love whoever is around to be loved."—**Kurt Vonnegut**
(writer, thought leader)

Being human has never been easy. Life on this planet does not come with an entitlement to feeling good. We innately want to believe there is something beyond the struggle we know here on Earth. Historically, religion has given us a sense of safety, structure, belonging, and certainty as we navigated life's difficulties. Today, we turn to television, alcohol, and all-inclusive resorts, which wouldn't be so popular if it were easy to achieve well-being. The point of building resilience and well-being is so that we can create for ourselves a sense of meaning and purpose, as well as a connection to something greater than ourselves. The feeling of belonging we seek comes with a sustainable relationship with the natural world around us, our original source of life. Only we, as individuals, can discover how best to nurture this relationship in today's changing world.

All of my suggestions thus far—from building community to eating well and sleeping more—take effort. None of those suggestions is an easy, miracle cure; some days, you won't feel like doing what you're doing or won't do it, or it won't feel good. Coping and building well-being are often like taking a vitamin; we may not see immediate evidence of its benefit, but we keep taking it as we know it is doing us good internally. It is much like going to work or school; despite the pains or monotony, we keep showing up because we want the end result of our efforts. Self-care is like putting puzzle pieces together as you decide what works for you. You're looking to build your mind, body, and spirit up so the hard times aren't quite as hard and the easier times are even worthier of celebration.

It must be acknowledged that effective coping mechanisms are more accessible to some than to others, and that privilege often results in a faster route to resilience. Some of the tools suggested may work for you; others may not work or may not be needed. What works for you changes throughout life and throughout different grief cycles. Outline a plan of action, do the work, then re-evaluate. Recreate the plan and keep trying—one day, one step, one habit at a time. This is the reality of grief work and life in a messy, complicated, unstable world. The goal is not to rid ourselves of all suffering; that is impossible anyway. The goal is to hold truth, responsibility, hope, and love all together.

Coping is about loving yourself so you can give love. You are likely reading this book because you want to do what's right and to be a good person. When I frame everything I do in this way, I release a lot of anxiety and guilt by accepting that the most I can do is my best in the moment. All I can expect from myself is to be present enough to give what I can, and to ensure I am taking care of myself. Let go of the "not good enough" guilt, and let go of the rigidity of trying to control other people. Lead with love. Far more effective than control, love will take you a long way in healing and will invite others to join you.

4
WHERE DO WE GO FROM HERE?

"The most difficult thing is the decision to act. The rest is merely tenacity."—**Amelia Earhart** (writer and first female aviator to cross the Atlantic Ocean solo)

We've reviewed the basics of climate change—the science as well as psychological tendencies that can get in the way of our appropriately tackling climate change. We've gotten to know climate grief and toured the stages of denial, anger, bargaining, sadness, acceptance, and meaning making. We've harnessed various tools for strengthening resilience and well-being, with an emphasis on the key role of community as well as individual physical health, mindfulness, and therapy. Through this process, we show ourselves the strength we have to create a healthy life in this challenging time.

Where do we go from here? We know that creating meaning around our grief grounds us in what matters—and that meaning comes alive through action. Investing in our climate awareness and strategizing for our well-being take us partway to where we need to go. Self-care itself has a positive effect, increasing our fitness to care for others and contributing to sustainable living.

But to be a part of the solutions to global problems, we must also focus on our responsibility to the world around us. There is so much more we can do to fight the continuing damage of climate change. Let us return to the urgent matter of how to combat climate change itself from a place of compassion for ourselves and others.

Animal Sanctuaries as a Model for Healthy Community Development

In 2010, I was a school counselor working with middle school kids. My students and I regularly shared our concerns for the environment and our frustration that the school's administration was ignoring innovative ideas for creating a more Earth-friendly campus. Every attempt at reducing plastic, increasing recycling, composting, building outdoor classroom space, or changing lunch menus was an uphill battle. If these extremely engaged kids weren't empowered to improve their own small school, I worried there really was no hope to change communities, corporations, or governments.

Compelled to seek out more tools for change, I started my doctoral journey at Prescott College, with a focus on social and environmental justice. Accompanied by twenty other professionals from different fields from around the world, I embarked on a PhD program to figure out how to inspire schools to follow their students' eco-friendly lead. In hindsight, I was also seeking to create meaning and purpose from my own climate grief, to feel less isolation and frustration. Fortunately, my classmates—equally desperate to create a viable action plan against climate change—brought so much optimism and drive to our discussions. I felt better than I had in a long time, having found my place in such a progressive community of thinkers and innovators.

I decided to study nonprofits as models for healthy community development. I wanted to find out what it took for a service-driven organization to be financially, socially, and environmentally sustainable. In business, the triple bottom line denotes a company's ability to generate a positive impact in all of three areas: profit, people, and the planet. In the nonprofit world, there is a fourth bottom line: the primary stakeholder, human or nonhuman, for whom we organize. I was first learning about animal sanctuaries as part of my research when I heard about a particularly successful street-animal rescue organization in India. Since I would be moving to India for a brief teacher exchange program, I decided to visit the rescue while I was there. From there, I was introduced to the vast network of animal rescues and sanctuaries.

Animal sanctuaries are organizations that rescue, rehabilitate, and house animals who have been neglected, abused, injured, or sent to slaughter. These sanctuaries' fourth bottom line is nature's most forgotten individuals. Nonhuman animals are victims of our lifestyles through deforestation, factory farming, animal research, abuse, poaching, pollution, and global warming. As the human population soared and the number of animals bred and killed in industrial farming exceeded seventy billion per year, wild animal populations have crashed. Sanctuaries have come on the scene to preserve what wildlife we have left, rescue domesticated animals from abuse, and educate the public. Because of their direct connection to nature, animal sanctuaries tend to have a high concern for their surrounding environment. They also have an extremely difficult financial model, as their primary stakeholders—animals—cannot give or make them money. Animal-focused organizations receive just a small fraction of total funding in the nonprofit sector. People who are attracted to working with animals in these organizations often have to tolerate very low pay and are susceptible to compassion fatigue and burnout, making this work even more difficult. The quadruple bottom line of sufficient animal care, positive impact for people, financial margins that make the work possible, and stewardship of the ecosystem is a formidable target to hit.

Even so, there are organizations doing so well that their influence is worldwide. Farm Sanctuary became famous as America's first farmed-animal sanctuary and now has multiple locations, including one established by Jon and Tracy Stewart. Some sanctuaries, or individual animals who live at sanctuaries, have become internationally known social media influencers. For example, Esther the Wonder Pig, a huge house-dwelling pig, began winning the world over in 2012 with her antics, hilariously captured by her human caretakers. The last few decades have seen a huge increase in the number of sanctuaries and the number of celebrities endorsing them or supporting related causes. Unfortunately, the number of animals in need has also skyrocketed.

To survive financially while providing for numerous animals, sustaining a community of engaged humans, and ensuring environmental sustainability takes extremely well-coordinated efforts. The work is physically demanding, emotionally taxing, and expensive. Whatever these sanctuaries' sustainability practices were, I assumed they could be applied to the fight against climate change and the collective battle with climate grief. For more than a year, I learned everything I could about the animal sanctuary world.

I studied more than two hundred sanctuaries around the world, practically memorizing their websites, comparing their programs, analyzing their financial reports, and looking at their multi-year trends. From there, I surveyed thirty-five of the most sustainable organizations. I asked them about their staffing trends, their volunteer base, how they found and maintained financial support, how they hoped to grow. Finally, I conducted case studies at four sanctuaries and have since volunteered at more than twenty others. What I found in common among sustainable sanctuaries were a similar pattern of collaborative work, a culture of hope and commitment, and truly inspiring stories. Here is what we can take away from their successes in order to be our most effective in mitigating climate change.

Collaboration over Competition

"We all do better when we all do better."—**Paul Wellsone**
(academic, progressive political leader)

In my study, the most interesting similarity that I found among successful animal sanctuaries was their focus on collaboration rather than competition—a refreshing break from the ubiquitous capitalistic message that competition is how we improve, that only winners have earned their keep. Capitalistic values have distorted our definition of success such that we think the threat of losing is the only thing that motivates us to do well. From work promotion, family game nights, sports, to social media following, we are conditioned to be competitive in so many aspects of our lives. But that was not the case at these animal sanctuaries.

In 2020, at the start of the pandemic, I was part of a team working to secure funding for animal sanctuaries. As the world went remote, sanctuaries suffered from the cancellation of visits and programs. Even when funding came to a halt, animal care certainly did not. An idea involving remote tours and introductions of animals went viral, and "Goats-to-Meeting" events were born. Corporations and schools called to schedule a visit from a sanctuary animal, generating funds for sanctuaries.

The initiative became a huge hit within weeks of the start of the pandemic. While the idea came from one sanctuary, that sanctuary made sure to include several others. Together, they created a hub for interested customers and managed the inflow as one large network of separate organizations. It was a beautiful display of their collaborative spirit.

From elementary school, we learn that competition motivates us to be our best. But consider how many times you have given up on a hobby because you knew you'd never be the best at it, or how many intriguing classes you didn't take because you didn't think you were good enough to try. My experience with competition has been that it shames, embarrasses, and intimidates far more than it motivates. Competition results in more wasted potential, more perceived failure, and more corruption—exactly what we *don't* need during times of ecological crisis. We must let go of this false and damaging value we place on competition, which actually impedes personal and community development and leads to wildly irresponsible use of natural resources. Instead, we can build a more sustainable society founded upon the antithesis of competition. Organizations like the animal sanctuaries I studied—those that create a sustainable business model based on collaboration—create holistic wealth for themselves and their communities.

Being in Community

> "Rarely, if ever, are any of us healed in isolation. Healing is an act of communion."—**bell hooks** (inspiring feminist, author, academic, activist)

While writing most of this book, I lived in San Diego. I enjoyed daily temperatures that made it seem like I was always in a cozy living room, took work breaks to watch swimming dolphins, and savored mid-winter patio dining. Every day felt like a vacation. I wasn't getting much writing done, but I was learning to surf, rollerblading along the bay, and meeting other young people who were enjoying the active lifestyle I'd dreamed of before moving to California. Eventually, though, I realized that while I loved my daily life there, I was struggling to recreate the sense of community I had left behind in Minnesota. I ultimately decided to move back to Minnesota, where so many people I collaborate with live. The roots I had there would have taken time and energy to replicate; I was actively feeling their absence. Immediately after moving back, I finished this book and started another. While I wasn't living a fun life that felt like a vacation every day, I was accomplishing the goals I felt responsible for, with the support of my community.

Wherever you are, consider how you can build community. Maybe online communities work best for you, or maybe you do best with a small in-person circle you have already curated. Whatever the level or type of community, build and maintain a community you can thrive in, as it will help you feel connected, supported, and inspired. Find other climate activists in particular. Buffer yourself from loneliness and isolation in any way that works for you. My best option was to return to my roots, and as soon as I did, my community worked magic for me. If you build your community of support just as sustainable organizations have built theirs, the same results will become reality for you.

The animal sanctuaries I studied are masters at being part of a community. They measure their capacity by how they can do the most good for the most stakeholders (including staff). The most holistically sustainable sanctuaries prioritize ensuring that everybody involved is benefiting from their experience. They encourage self-care, assertiveness, conflict resolution, and slowing down so that they can make sound decisions as a group and so that everybody feels heard and understood. I saw just how much attention they paid to protecting volunteers and ensuring inclusion. I heard from staff members who were happy with vacation time, opportunities for learning and advancement, and a company culture marked by special events, freedom of expression, and equity policies. By contrast, sanctuaries that did not seem to have a healthy culture among their people struggled with turnover, financial instability, and negative public impression.

The more years I have spent in the workforce, the more I have realized that sadly, concern for staff satisfaction is uncommon. Too often, staff become tools for financial gain instead of teammates with common goals. The best-functioning animal sanctuaries prioritize staff well-being as an obvious part of community health. Do you treat yourself like an overworked staff member for your agenda? I know I have in the past, and have had to leave jobs as I worked on prioritizing my real needs rather than pushing myself as if my goals were more important than my own body. Life shouldn't feel like a contest, and we certainly shouldn't be competing against our own well-being for success. The best lesson I learned from collaborative and community-driven animal sanctuaries is that we all do better when we don't leave each other, or a part of ourselves, behind.

Positivity

Positivity attracts positivity. The organizations I studied that had the strongest circle of donors and volunteers, inspired the most excitement around them, and were able to find support when they needed it were those that led with positivity. This is not to say that we should not be honest about bad situations, but celebrating all positive news, no matter how small, is a great way to build a cheering section. Research backs this up: many studies, from market research to psychological studies, suggest that people feel drained by a constant onslaught of bad, urgent, and dire news. While it is true that dwelling on sorrows can garner sympathy, individuals who do this tend to disempower themselves and remain stuck in a victim mentality, and organizations that do this tend to wear down their support systems. The balance we should look for is embodied by truth-based positivity, because there is always some positivity in what is true. Even if your circumstances are terrible, you can choose integrity, self-discipline, humor, and community. Look for newsworthy progress to share with your people—and go create some yourself.

Again, this is vastly different from toxic positivity. Toxic positivity is just as dishonest as constant self-victimization. That's what makes it toxic: it's a lie, a manipulation of reality, and it cheapens the real human experience. Even in bad times, wherever you can find a source for levity or joy, embrace it, along with the reality of the struggle. Embrace the reality of the situation and simultaneously hold any appreciation you can. Organizations that do this attract others to join them, which results in more opportunities to build upward. This looks like social media posts that are usually lighthearted, fun, silly, and celebratory, with calls for action being the exception rather than the norm. There is certainly a time and place for sharing hardships and needs, sadness and bad news. Sometimes, in the life of an organization, like in our own lives, dark times and times of hardship happen. In those times, the community will show up as trust has been built over time as part of an honest and empowering relationship.

At the same time as you express positivity, shape your mindset by consuming good news. Stop allowing yourself to dwell on bad news, dramatic television programming, or violence, which can heighten stress and negative emotions. There is no need to engage with a movie that ramps up your anxiety or to doom-scroll past a bunch of sensationalized headlines. Consume only what you need or really want, what is good for you, what leaves you feeling adequately informed, inspired, or relaxed. We are surrounded by both tragedy and joy every day. Mindfully choose your focus.

The organizations I studied grew from individuals who were committed to collaborating with each other to create a place of hope and healing. They took an overwhelming, dire, and often hopeless situation and responded with compassion, effort, and positivity. Having met so many organizational founders and leaders, I have come to realize that these visionaries' personal goals and approaches to life greatly informed how their organizations would operate. This realization inspired new ideas and brought new life to my work as a therapist and to my attempts at coping with my own grief.

It took me months of reflection on what I had learned at the sanctuaries before I was able to identify ways to integrate the lessons of active hope and positivity, collaborative community building, and holistic sustainability into my own life. What came out of this, however, was a new approach that I continue to use in both my professional and personal life.

Nature-Based Therapeutic Service
"Let your heart crumble into an infinite amount of tiny, precious seeds. Then plant love everywhere you go."
—**Anita Krizzan** (writer)

My dissertation led me to a new therapeutic framework for daily living and community building. To explain it, I will first return to ecopsychology. Ecopsychology is the study centered around how humans can healthfully interact with nature, just like ecotherapy, its therapeutic practice equivalent.[1] Ecopsychology asks these questions: *How do humans and nature affect each other? How does it feel to be surrounded by healthy nature? How does it feel to be surrounded by unhealthy nature or a sterile and unnatural environment? How do we feel when nonhuman animals interface with us? How do we feel when we help them? What is our relationship with or responsibility to nature and other animals?* As mentioned earlier, I was first interested in this area of study back when it was invisible to the rest of the psychology field; even my graduate-level professors did not know to direct me to ecopsychology. When I finally learned about the discipline during my PhD program, I quickly came to appreciate that ecopsychology (and ecotherapy) offered insight into the connections between our emotional experience and our natural surroundings as well as our relationship with nature. Climate grief is not a surprise or mystery to ecotherapists. Ecotherapy offers restorative strategies for combatting both climate grief and climate change.

Eager to bring ecopsychology principles to life for myself and my community, I designed a therapeutic strategy to use with my mental health clients, inspired especially by Theadore Roszak's assertion that "the goal of Ecopsychology is to awaken the inherent sense of environmental reciprocity that lies within the ecological unconscious." My understanding was that I could offer clients a tool for personal healing that also helped heal the planet. To do this, I simply combined the time we spent on traditional talk therapy with time spent outside engaging with nature. We would garden, care for chickens, pull invasive plants from the woods, dig rain gardens, count monarch butterfly cocoons, and create sustainable living goals. I refer to my approach as *nature-based therapeutic service*—a service that is very intentionally beneficial for both nature and ourselves.

I had found similar programs at some of the sanctuaries I studied. *Care farming*, common in Europe, is a type of program wherein students with special needs learn various skills on the farm as they develop a healthy relationship with animals and nature. Comparable programs in North America offer children opportunities to play and learn in nature or at farms. *Wilderness therapy*, wherein clients are brought into the wild for an immersive experience, has similar objectives. Practices that foster meaning making, tangible improvements in the natural world and the skills necessary to create these changes, and therapeutic progress for the client will promote planetary and personal healing. I found that the habits I was building in doing this work with my clients, beyond its promise as a therapeutic approach, were helping me establish a healthier and more sustainable life that better reflected my hopes for a sustainable world.

First, I applied nature-based service to my travels. Having always loved to travel, I felt guilty about the immense amounts of fossil fuels burned for every flight I took. Doing some sort of nature-based service wherever I visited helped me offset the carbon burden, create a personal connection to new places, and give much-needed assistance to the organizations I visited. With my experience at animal sanctuaries, I began seeking out sanctuaries wherever I went, offering days of experienced help. It has been such a positive experience! I noticed I love to travel even more. I felt like a global citizen and like I was truly doing something good for the world that was unique to my skills and interests. I got to play with an Andean (spectacled) bear cub, who awoke in me a sense of reverence for bears. I took care of an orphaned spider monkey and a capuchin, both of whom were as eager to interact with and learn from me as I was eager to learn from them. I cleaned stalls at several overwhelmed farm sanctuaries. I helped veterinarians transport a sick horse. I washed the itching skin of dogs suffering from severe mange. I fed baby squirrels. I bore witness as animals passed on and, sometimes being the only person there, ensured they were as comfortable as possible. I cried with their caretakers and handled paperwork while people mourned. While it is difficult work emotionally and physically, I have never felt more fulfilled in my work or more connected to this planet and to other humans than when I am helping out at animal sanctuaries.

Next, I applied nature-based service to my daily home life. I became obsessed with how to turn my tiny urban property into a model for sustainable living. I installed solar panels, a rain garden, and pollinator-friendly plants. I bought used furniture, changed up my typical grocery shopping with jars and bulk bin goods, and found joy in trying new sustainable habits every month. The key to doing this therapeutically is that along the way, I noticed what helped me feel good. If a new idea was too expensive, time-consuming, or difficult to implement, or if it left me feeling drained, I didn't do it! Every choice I made was based on this core question: *would this action serve both myself and nature?* This framing brought my grief work, my self-care strategies, and my sustainability goals all into line with each other. This was holistic sustainability. Just as sustainable nonprofits can maintain a quadruple bottom line—prioritizing people, the planet, profitability, and their primary stakeholders all at once—we can take a similar approach to our lives.

Creating a Holistically Sustainable Lifestyle

"It's very hard to have ideas. It's very hard to put yourself
out there, it's very hard to be vulnerable, but those people
who do that are the dreamers, the thinkers, and the
creators. They are the magic people of the world."

—**Amy Poehler** (comedian, actress, writer)

The way to have a holistically sustainable lifestyle is simply to create habits that help yourself and nature. The important thing is to make sure that you accept what you are doing as good and let yourself build on your success rather than berate yourself about the pace of your progress. You do not need any certificate or degree, or external assistance to create this therapeutic lifestyle for yourself (though if you have the means and desire to make use of coaching, classes, therapists, or mentors, it can certainly help). It takes some effort to craft a new approach to living, but in the end, it will directly influence both your grief and the climate. Having already laid out strategies for self-care and well-being and learned about sustainable organizational development, now we will consider more direct actions that both support our own health and amplify our efforts to curb climate change.

As you read the following section, build your goals around what you enjoy doing and learning. Consider what strategies can sustainably fit into your lifestyle. What worked for me was getting involved with animal sanctuaries and spending time and effort on the physical space of my home. But sustainability will not look the same for everybody. We are not all cut out to clean stalls and care for potentially dangerous animals. Had I not been trained and prepared for the work at a sanctuary, my volunteering would have been a burden to an already overworked and under-resourced team of people. Likewise, not everybody wants homeownership or homesteading, and housing prices often aren't within reach of people who do. My two primary strategies for contributing to sustainability may not be relevant to you, and some of the following suggestions also may not resonate with you. Take the information that helps you move forward with your own unique strategies. Dr. Lindsey Rudibaugh, my colleague at Prescott College and co-founder of Tenderfoot Learning Lab (a center for sustainable living education), tells her students to "help the way you're needed." Understand your own needs and preferences, establish your own self-care and wellness routine, and then look for compatible opportunities. The best strategies help everybody involved.

Systems Thinking

Systems thinking refers to how we can understand a problem and establish solutions in a way that takes into account the entire web of stakeholders connected to the situation.[2] Systems thinking is the exploration of interrelationships and perspectives that give a situation its complexity. Within every situation is a system of interacting factors, and a complex situation is understood only when seen in its entirety. For example, consider the system connected to a peanut butter and jelly sandwich. I, the eater, see only the few components that make up my lunch. But also connected to this sandwich are farmers who picked the berries, grew the peanuts, and harvested the wheat. There are distributors and truck drivers, and grocery store workers. Then there is my friend, sitting next to me in the coffee shop, who is concerned about her own peanut allergy. Every relationship, every decision, every situation we find ourselves in can be better understood through systems thinking.

Consider an important relationship in your life right now. When a miscommunication arises, it is because of a series of decisions, feelings, reactions, misunderstandings, and other factors. You and the other party each have your own valid experience of the situation, and to understand the situation completely requires both of you to be curious about the other's entire experience. That is the system of the relationship.

As you develop your next steps to fight climate change, start with a consideration of systems: systems of which you are a critical part (such as your family, romantic relationship, workplace) and systems around you which you aim to change (such as local transportation initiatives, city green spaces, flooding coastlines). We have already talked about sustainability as a system, about how our behaviors impact our own wellness and how our health is connected to the health of our communities. As we work to reduce our energy expenditure, to use fewer resources and create less waste, we can now go about it with the good of various social and ecological systems in mind.

Consider a decision you might make as part of a sustainable lifestyle, such as to get solar panels, sell your car, or switch to a vegan diet. Would this decision simply be carried out without causing a complex chain of effects? Of course not. Thinking through this chain of effects will help you decide your best next step. Let's say that you decide to sell your car and have your whole family ride bikes from now on. If it is not feasible for one member of your family to bike to work, you will have just greatly damaged an entire system (your household). When you think about a household, a workplace, or a community as a system, you are taking a holistic view of the given situation.[3]

Systems thinking can enhance every decision you make by showing you details you may have missed and helping you better understand others' perspectives. In graduate school, for a project, I had to study a single product, including the origins of each of its components, the resources used to create it, and its lifespan from production to consumption. The project encouraged me to be more cautious about what I used, and moreover, to decide to go fully plant-based, as I began to understand the workings of our food system and the harmful impacts of industrial farming—not just on animals but also on the planet, on workers, and on my own health. A choice that I had previously attributed simply to taste preferences gained a whole new meaning once I saw the whole system involved.

I feel more hope when I think about climate change through systems thinking, because I can appreciate the ripple effects of seemingly small actions and the influence just one person can have on an entire community. Consider learning more about systems thinking and practicing it, and I imagine you will begin to experience profound changes in your life. A helpful resource is Zoe Weil's book *Most Good Least Harm*, which, while it is not explicitly about systems thinking, helps the reader think through decisions in this way. Students and families can also use this book together.

Activism Your Own Way

The best part about a system is that it contains many components with different roles. If we think about the fight against climate change as a system, we can be confident that it takes many different approaches by many of us to succeed. The planet needs you not to do any one specific thing, but to do something. Maybe you already are an activist and feel confident about your contribution, but more likely, you are unsure of how best to contribute or even where to start. As I was building my career, it seemed to me that social and environmental justice activists led a life that was out of my reach. My long-held assumption that activists had something special made me believe I couldn't be one. The reality is that activists are regular people everywhere doing extraordinary work to make the world better. They are not necessarily more talented or skilled than the next person. They are not necessarily richer, smarter, or more privileged, and they are not all from families with long histories of activism. Of course, having privilege, financial stability, and direct access to role models helps. Activism is more difficult without these things, but it is never impossible. Activists are people who seek to understand systems of injustice and who continually make changes in their lives as they learn. Activists acknowledge that someone else isn't going to solve the world's problems for them, and they feel a sense of urgency and responsibility to take action. You are doing activism by thinking critically about the state of the world, aligning your lifestyle with your core values, and finding the best way (for you personally) to contribute to solutions.

Activism is not an all-or-nothing lifestyle. I assumed that to call myself an activist, I needed to have hit some magic combination of volunteering, sacrifice, and leadership. For many activists, activism is a full-time commitment, even a distinct lifestyle, but others' activism may be subtler. Our roles in fighting climate change are as different as our personalities; they also change over time as life circumstances dictate the resources we have to give. Often, unprecedented needs or concerns motivate us to be more active. Several studies show that since a recent presidential election, a large majority of Americans have participated in a protest, boycotted a company, signed a petition, or taken action in another way. Nowadays, with an increasing number of tools at our disposal, there are endless ways for us to get involved. The best actions for you to take are those that align your biggest concerns with your skills, interests, and resources.

Just keep taking the best next step. This mantra has enabled me to exit the state of overwhelm and finally engage in activism that fit me, to stop feeling self-conscious about whether I was doing it "right." In one of my favorite TED talks, Erika Abrams, who, with her family, founded Animal Aid Unlimited, the sanctuary I visited in India, recounted her family's experience of trying to help one street dog. Shocked by the sheer number of street animals in need, they nevertheless felt helpless and unsure of where to start. That was when a friend told Erika: "Do something. Just don't do nothing." That really is the secret to success, whether you consider yourself an activist, or you're trying to reduce your own footprint on the planet, or you've just begun coping with climate grief. You do not need to do everything. Just don't do nothing.

The Rs of Sustainability

Waste is a big part of our environmental problems. In December 2020, the world officially reached a sad tipping point: there was now more human-created mass on the planet than there was natural biomass—our produced materials now outweighed nature.[4] While some of the products we use are necessary and long-lasting, many (especially most plastic products) are unnecessary or are meant for single use. The more our culture embraces throw-away, convenience commodities, the more unnatural bulk we add to the planet in the form of materials that were garbage to begin with.

The "Reduce, Reuse, Recycle" slogan was popularized in the 1970s as the need for environmental conservation gained attention. The goal of the 3-R slogan was to put a stop to mindless overconsumption by urging people to consume less and reuse what they could, as well as to recycle materials, where possible, at the end of their current life. This was a good start, as more Rs have now been added, including "refuse," "repurpose," "refill," "regift," "rethink," and others.

It is not hard to intuit the merits of refusing, reusing, reducing, repurposing, and reinventing, or to understand why doing anything with used materials is better than buying a new product. Yet, most of us struggle to put these lessons into practice consistently. It is simply really convenient not to. It takes effort to override our desire for convenience, to double down on our motivation, and to replace old habits with greener ones, one day at a time. Of course, our lifestyles are all different, so the ways in which we might realign our consumption habits can't be uniform. That is the beauty of thinking about our lifestyles using the various Rs: they are not a specific prescription but a framework. A framework for living that is healthy and aligned with our personal goals, though, does take effort, since it is not what society expects of us. The overwhelming focus on recycling at the expense of the other Rs is a great example of how we gravitate toward the habit change that is the most convenient, regardless of whether it is actually conducive to our end goal.

Recycle

"There are a thousand hacking at the branches of evil to one who is striking at the root."—**Henry David Thoreau**
(social justice activist, naturalist, and philosopher)

Recycling is the first image that comes to mind when we think of sustainable living; for many, it is where sustainability starts and ends. Though the original message of "Reduce, Reuse, Recycle" suggested recycling as a last resort, recycling has been treated like a salve for consumer guilt. Contrary to popular belief, the recycling symbol on plastic products, born out of the first

Earth Day as a means of promoting sustainability goals, does not actually indicate whether a material is recyclable. Unfortunately, many mistakenly believe that the symbol alone means something is recyclable regardless of the number attached to it (not the case) and that recycling is a great alternative to throwing something in the garbage (also not always the case). Plastics do not have a simple life. Their production is resource-intensive; most plastics are not recyclable, and even those that are recyclable are not recycled easily or efficiently.

The number inside the circular symbol, ranging from 1 to 7, tells the consumer what type of plastic something is and whether it can be accepted in their jurisdiction. Even when the number indicates that an item cannot be recycled, many still resort to *wish-cycling*—tossing the item into the recycling bin anyway with the hope that it will somehow work. I've had that thought: *I'd like this wrapper/container not to go straight to landfill. Maybe it's okay that it's dirty or a weird material, or that it once contained a toxic cleaning chemical.* But the reality is that any unrecyclable item we toss into the recycling bin puts the rest of that bin's contents at risk of not getting recycled at all. Staff at the recycling center can do only so much sorting. Dirty, non-recyclable objects often take other, perfectly recyclable objects with them to the landfill. But even when we are recycling only legitimately recyclable materials, recycling is not the effective solution we want it to be. Creating plastic is expensive, requiring water, oil, and other materials, yet recycling plastic is often just as costly, when possible at all. Recycling paper is better than producing more, but the process requires a lot of water. Recyclable metals, like cans, have a simpler recycling process. Keep recycling, but only recycle materials that your local center can process, and make sure to clean them before tossing them in the bin.

Refuse and Reduce

To maintain or reduce the amount of stuff one owns is to engage in a constant battle against cultural norms. It takes practice to get used to questioning every purchase and deciding whether it is a need or a want, whether it's the best option or whether there are less wasteful alternatives. Our ability to buy everything online has only exacerbated mindless consumption. The more we buy, the more our demand justifies continued production.

Everything that is made comes with an environmental cost. Consider the materials that go into each product: trees, mined minerals, water, and energy all get more and more depleted with each thing we shop for. We'd realize how much less we need if we peer-pressured each other into refusing and reducing rather than constantly buying more to keep up with trends. Do we need two sets of dishes if one will just sit around gathering dust most of the year? Do we need a living room *and* a study, *and* a family room, *and* a TV room in the basement? Do we need our own truck, or can we borrow from a friend as needed? We can reduce consumption in many areas of daily living if we are willing to look critically at what we actually use.

When I plan on buying something, I ask myself the following questions: *Do you have something else you can repurpose? If you waited a week, would you still want or need it? Would you even remember wanting it? Would you feel better about refusing than about having it? Instead of buying it new, can you buy it used? Can you borrow it?* If, after these questions, I still feel a need for the thing I'm buying, I let myself buy it without guilt. Your habits for sustainability also have to be a sustainable part of your lifestyle; don't get stuck overthinking necessary, helpful, or desired purchases.

Reuse, Repurpose, and Reinvent

My friends are always inspiring me with countless ideas to reuse, repurpose, and reinvent stuff I own. When cleaning out my closet, I used to pack clothes I no longer wanted to bring to a thrift shop, then quickly refill the empty space. Then a friend told me that she would store unwanted clothes away for reconsideration in a few months and found that she would happily pull things back out to wear again. I also found out that another friend of mine would collect containers to repurpose as plant pots around the house, which made me realize how often we keep multiple items with the same function in our homes. Sometimes, things we grow tired of just need a facelift, or a break, or a new job. Sometimes, swapping similar items with friends can offer us the same emotional gratification as a new purchase. Clothing swaps and vintage shops are having a moment, but to actually reuse what we have, to adopt repurposing and reinvention as our default options rather than just supplement our regular shopping with unnecessary thrifting is a learned habit that takes effort to build. Nonetheless, we can make it a joyful habit.

Need ideas, inspiration, or accountability partners? Invite friends to a *sustainability party*. Decide if you'll do a kitchen swap, an unused beauty supplies swap, an idea swap, or whatever else would help you start a new habit together. If your closest friends know you have a goal of living more sustainably, you'll create within your social circle a culture that prioritizes healthy social habits, valuing swapping over shopping or walks over happy hours. It will be a fun way to *realign* together with your community so you aren't trying to create new habits alone.

Search around the internet for tips and hacks from the many awesome sustainability experts who offer them online. Pick out a few new Rs to try. Remember: recycling is the bare minimum, so if you don't yet recycle, now is a great time to start, but push yourself further. My favorite R is "rethink." Rethink your daily habits, your worries or reluctance around change, and your assumptions about what your social circle might be open to. It might seem like there are so many habits to break or there is not enough support. Make this endeavor fun for yourself and an invigorating challenge for your family and friends. Before you know it, new habits will form, and you'll be naturally building momentum for more.

Setting a Sustainable Table

I recognize the majesty of trees
towering pines
cover the sky
on branches where the monarchs lie
your birch bark canoe gonna take us to
that island where the palm trees sway
it's a fantasy
it's lost at sea
as the Amazon dies for your beef
—"Majesty of Beasts," poem-turned-song by **Mary Bue**
(musician, writer, teacher)

The busier we are, the more likely we are to practice unsustainable habits in our day-to-day lives without knowing it. We eat more packaged food for the sake of convenience. We use our vehicles and electronics more. We are more active after dark, requiring more electricity. We adopt more and more shortcuts for basic maintenance, creating additional waste: Clorox wipes instead of cloth and homemade cleaning liquids, drying laundry in dryers instead of hang-drying outside, microwaving dinners in single-use, plastic packaging instead of cooking big pots of vegetables from our own gardens. Rethinking food is one way to push back against this reality since we spend so much of our daily lives eating. Reclaiming home cooking, healthy ingredients, and sit-down dinner time can let us move away from fast-paced, convenience eating and back into a more quality- and sustainability-focused eating routine.

Food is a necessary part of life and an important part of most people's personal and cultural experiences. We eat several times a day and each have unique preferences and habits; nearly every holiday in every culture is accompanied by food traditions; and each family has special recipes or memorable dishes. Small changes in eating habits go a long way as they are compounded daily, several times a day, generating an enormous difference over time. Thus, rethinking our lifestyles for sustainability means rethinking food. As discussed in Chapter 3, our eating habits should be an expression of self-care, and this care naturally extends to the planet. Setting a sustainable table includes considering which foods we buy, where they came from, how they were grown and harvested, how we cook them, and where the leftovers go.

Which foods are local, sustainably sourced, ethically harvested, and easier on the budget will depend on your location and other factors. Most foods have more sustainable and less sustainable options, such as organic versus non-organic fruits or imported potatoes versus potatoes grown for a local market. Personal circumstances also dictate your options regarding health food stores, composting, gardening, farming, and so on. Think of your options as a continuum from baseline to better to best so as to avoid feeling like foods are either "bad" or "good." Disordered eating is a common problem in our culture, and a dietary shift for sustainability should be something that brings joy and health rather than shame and unhealthy restriction.

What to Eat

"Part of the urgency we feel with food arises from the reality that it has so many ramifications on our planet, beyond whether or not we are eating other animals. This means every choice counts. . . . Factors ranging from treatment of workers, to environmental impact, to access to food, and much more are all crucial considerations we have to make if we truly care about just food."—**lauren Ornelas** (social justice activist, founder of Food Empowerment Project)

Foods lower on the food chain are more naturally abundant, easier to source locally, and gentler on both our bodies' digestive systems and the planet's ecosystem. Plant-based foods are low on the food chain and, as discussed, constitute a diet on which humans can thrive. A plant-based diet is better environmentally because it takes out the middle consumer—other animals. The animals we eat all require food, water, and shelter; the farmland used to feed and house them could instead be used to grow food for humans, creating a more direct and efficient path for the calories to get to our plates. Given how much agricultural land is dedicated to feeding livestock, based on resource use alone, plant-based eating is the eco-friendlier option. The amount of water required to produce plant milk, even when we consider the most water-intensive crop, pales in comparison to that required to produce cow's milk. The massive number of calories a cow needs to consume to grow large enough for slaughter dwarfs the number of calories in their meat. Furthermore, the waste generated by the factory farming industry is extremely taxing on the planet, polluting the air, making the water toxic, eroding the soil and depleting it of nutrients. Remember to consider the system connected to each product. Animals raised for meat on local farms are often still given non-local feed; certain fruits and vegetables are still available only from industrial farms far away. Determine your options based on your situation.

Among the endless possibilities to examine as you shift your eating habits, your better options and best options will surface as you consider your location, health concerns, preferences, finances, and time budget. It might take more time and money to eat better. If you have the resources, this is an important investment. We are talking about the most intimate connection you have to the world around you. The stuff you put into your body is what creates necessary cells, tissues, and fluids in the days and weeks to come. Do you want your body to be created from health or from disease?

Over the past four years, I have been slowly turning my yard, a quarter-acre plot in the middle of a small city, into a food supply. There are apple, cherry, and plum trees that are starting to produce fruit, some berry bushes and a grape vine that have established themselves, and in late summer, the vegetable garden produces plenty of tomatoes, peppers, greens, and beans. I am a long way from sustaining myself on food from my yard alone, but with more time and learning, I can see myself getting there. To supplement your *yarden* (a yard growing food instead of grass!), or if you don't have the time or space to grow your own food, support *community-supported agriculture* (CSA) operations—farms that are local, often organic or chemical-free, sustainably sized, and in relationship with their community. Through CSAs, you get locally produced foods while directly supporting farmers. I enjoy supplementing the fruits of my own food-growing attempts with produce from a CSA throughout the summer. In the winter, I buy more from my local food co-op. Food cooperatives are grocery stores that, while sporting generally higher price tags than do big-box chain grocers, have higher standards for the companies they work with. To meet your social as well as dietary needs, look for local restaurants with locavore or plant-based offerings. Choosing to eat foods that will best feed yourself and the planet is a constant but empowering exercise, and one that gets easier as you go along.

How to Eat

Believe it or not, your kitchen offers almost as many choices as does your grocery shopping. Cooking and food storage both require energy. You may be in a position to improve energy use in the kitchen if you can upgrade appliances or are the person who cooks or manages the food supply. Ideally, we would all stock our kitchens with energy-efficient appliances powered by renewable energy. However, most of us can already do a lot within the confines of our current situation.

Here are the easiest ways to curb energy use. Keeping a refrigerator stocked instead of mostly empty reduces the energy it needs to keep cool. Eating cold meals in warm weather, on days when the air conditioning may be on, eliminates the use of the stove or oven. Always eating food before it expires cuts the amount of food that gets tossed before it's even consumed. If you have old appliances, make sure they are running well; when you don't need to use an appliance, unplug it. If you decide to redesign your kitchen or add kitchen tools, do research on the current best options. The last few decades have seen the rise and fall of natural gas, once the cause of much excitement and now universally recognized as an unsustainable addition to the kitchen. How we prepare and store food, not just which foods we eat, matters for our carbon footprint. Habits, rituals, and traditions around cooking food are highly specific to each individual; the most sustainable habits you can come up with will be those that feel right to *you*.

Where Food Waste Goes

About half of all the food we buy ends up in the garbage, completely unconsumed. This is a huge issue, both for the planet and for our wallets, but also a very fixable one. Planning ahead is one solution, but also consider what happens when you do throw food away. Does it go in the garbage, or do you compost? Composting is one of the most important habits we can create, with so much of our soil becoming depleted of nutrients. Compost returns nutrition to the soil and produces more soil instead of taking up space in the landfill, where it contributes only to methane production. If we also stop consuming animal products, there's the added bonus of being able to compost almost everything on our plates. Some neighborhoods offer curbside compost collection or a community collection site. Research the best way forward given your situation and location. I promise: with enough creativity, even apartment dwellers can find a way to compost. When I am traveling or staying in an apartment, I store compostable food waste in the freezer, then bring it to a community compost site. Whenever I have lived somewhere long enough to establish a composting habit, I have managed to create a system, even in apartments with limited space. It does take some time to set up such a system and to get into the habit of using it, but you'll be encouraged when you get to make use of the beautiful soil it produces. In any case, the worst thing you can do is throw food away to rot in a landfill, its nutrients completely removed from the soil forever. Composting also gets a bad reputation because people think compost is stinky and difficult to manage, but I have found neither to be true. Check out how often food is going to waste in your household so that you can realign your shopping habits, create a compost space, and establish food goals that take into account the entire life cycle of your food.

Population and Reproduction

As of 2022, the human population has doubled since the first Earth Day in 1970. Never has a species grown so quickly globally, with such impact on the planet. Usually, when a population grows, its predators also increase in number or resources become too scarce to support it, and the population contracts again. But humankind's story has taken a far different turn. Throughout history, we have killed off all potential predators, hoarded more and more resources for ourselves, and kept expanding our range. By exploiting each other and damaging bioregions, we have managed to stretch beyond healthy limits, even as resources became more and more depleted.

In the decades leading up to 1970, American families had smaller houses, traveled less, ate less meat, and owned far fewer electronic devices. Food in the grocery store was more seasonally dictated. Clothing was often handmade rather than bought frequently and discarded quickly. People gardened more, and most farms were still small. Since then, we have resorted to mass deforestation to make room for both urban sprawl and industrial farmland, to accommodate a human population hurtling toward its current number of nearly 8 billion.

The incredible rate of human population growth has put a strain not only on nature but on ourselves. From the job market, cost of living, city traffic, to pollution, many facets of our lives have changed with the expansion of our numbers. Because our lifestyles now cost the planet more finite resources than ever, even maintaining our population at this point is unsustainable. We can work to reduce our carbon footprints with lifestyle changes, but it is probably impossible for a human to have a net negative carbon impact, and the only way for us to drive down our carbon use in time is through quick and drastic change. Population has to be considered.

Increasingly, parents and potential parents face feelings of guilt and concern for their children's future on this planet as climate change gets worse. The worry is that the next generation will witness a wide range of calamities, worse than anything so far; that pandemics will become more frequent, ocean acidification and pollution more severe, and air quality worse; that life will be a dystopian nightmare in the coming years and decades. Many potential parents hesitate and many current parents fear the worst as they consider what bringing a child into this world means, not just for the planet but for that child.

And yet, we have a hardwired desire to nurture, caretake, and possibly parent. Evolutionarily, this drive was about maintaining our species' population, but socially and emotionally, it is about so much more. Parenthood or the possibility of parenthood is ingrained in many cultural and religious structures, becoming a prominent part of our expectations of adulthood, even of our identity and, sadly, our self-worth. People often see their offspring as their legacy, as an opportunity to impart knowledge, fix past mistakes, and offer opportunities they and previous generations could not get. Many people really do feel an innate joy at the prospect of having and raising children, and their desire to pursue that is valid and worthy.

Still, as the global situation changes, so do younger generations' perspectives on parenthood. More women are waiting longer to get married and are having fewer children compared to previous generations. More are choosing not to have kids at all and instead find other ways to build a legacy, such as investing in their community. More couples are deeming the world too unstable and cannot justify having a child. Mounting economic stressors leave people feeling too uncertain to start a family; higher pressures in the workplace steer their attention toward their careers; and the cumulative effects of geo-political concerns lead to more ambiguity in family planning.

It is difficult for people to talk about this topic because it is so deeply personal yet comes with intense social pressure to follow the norm. Those who don't want to or can't have kids are often not given an emotionally safe space to share their perspectives without being judged. Having honest conversations about family planning as an ethically weighted choice takes a lot of sensitivity to a wide range of feelings and experiences. Indeed, the choice to have fewer or no children may challenge family traditions, and also the fundamentally capitalist belief that growth is inherently good and necessary. The planetary reality is that growth is neither inherently good nor sustainable. There simply is not room for every human to grow richer, have more offspring, own a bigger house, and take up more land and resources.

Since, fortunately, not everybody wants to have kids, it is quite possible that if given the autonomy and choice, we can establish a sustainable population and will have the resources to adequately support all children into the future. When I was still a teenager, I made the decision not to have biological children. It is not that I dislike kids, and I am neither jealous of nor indignant toward people who choose to have kids. In fact, choosing not to have children enables me to be more supportive of friends who do. I made my decision carefully, after weighing a variety of factors, from my own health, to my life goals, to the state of the planet. It felt right for me. If having children is no longer a cultural expectation, then the decision to do so becomes far more sacred and meaningful for everybody.

Procreation is so enmeshed in religious and cultural values the world over that shrinking populations are a cause for alarm. Fears of shrinking workforces and dying cultures drive the perspective that population growth is the only sign of progress. But this mindset reveals a failure to see the big picture. Just one hundred years ago, the human population was drastically smaller, yet there were more cultures around the world. Cultures usually die not because of a naturally shrinking population but because of colonization and urbanization. Indeed, humankind's population boom has diluted and destroyed rather than enriched cultures. Further, a population decrease would give us an opportunity to mindfully shape our workforce to reflect an intact community rather than a consumer-driven global economy. We could move our society away from an exploitative job market. We could halt our need for more clear-cut land, and we could slow our natural resource use. The myth of infinite economic growth as beneficial to all is simply not true in the experience of most people around the world.

Alleviating the cultural expectation for child rearing would allow people the time and space to critically consider their situation and goals. Indeed, there are alternatives to parenting that still let one play an important role in a child's life, as engendering a healthy multigenerational community involves mentoring and teaching, as well as nurturing relationships outside the nuclear family structure. On the other hand, for people who do want to parent but are concerned about the environment, mindful planning and dedication to resource management can help reduce their family's carbon footprint. If you are currently without a child and still unsure if or when you might want to have children, and how many, consider your options seriously and not so much expectations of you. If you decide to have kids, can you reduce your carbon footprint in other ways? Can you commit to less travel, grow more of your own food, or eat more plant-based? Can you commit to a smaller home or create a multigenerational home? If you already have kids, can you implement ways to build more sustainability into their daily habits? If you have friends who do not have kids, can you be sure your conversations are inclusive? If you do not have kids, can you offer support to friends who do? How can you create a healthy multigenerational community that focuses less on contributing to the GDP and more on holistic sustainability?

We can all experience a full life, and the deepest depths of love and purpose, regardless of our procreation status. If we consider climate change in deciding whether or how to parent, we will likely find a path that feels right, be it being childfree, having fewer children, or practicing environmentally mindful parenting. Regardless of the family structure one chooses, that choice is valid and should be honored. In this era of resource depletion, the decision not to have children could be applauded, as it allows childfree adults to contribute more to their community and bigger families to access more planetary resources. As more people elect to be childfree, do not fear for society. Our economy will be fine with a smaller workforce! After all, whom is an eternally growing economy really good for? Would it really be so bad if we had more balanced work lives and enough jobs to go around, could reduce homelessness and poverty, and didn't worry so much about GDP? Instead, it's time to be more concerned about national well-being scores.

Slow Down

One outcome of the COVID-19 lockdown was that most of us got a taste of a lifestyle of stillness. There was no longer the pressure, or even opportunity, to rush from one event to the next. We could not fill our schedules with social activities. Many of us had a chance to re-evaluate what was really important and to reduce our daily routine to a more manageable volume.

Climate change is all about energy storage, release, and consumption: burning fossil fuels to generate power releases previously stored carbon into the air. Think of your lifestyle in terms of energy. Living sustainably means you are not spending more than you have or will gain back, whether it is a natural resource or your own physical and mental energy. Everything we do is based on energy, from our bodily movements and activities, materials we build, to electricity and gasoline in our cars. Our energy is not infinite and is exchanged for finite amounts of money, skills, or opportunities. The cost of using energy is time and potential that could have gone toward something else. Slowing down enables us to be more deliberate and intentional, cutting back on any of those energy exchanges we do not need and saving that energy for a later opportunity.

How do we begin slowing down our lifestyles? Focus first on what matters most. Think critically about what matters to you and why, and cut out anything that is unimportant or unhealthy, or that in any way contributes to more harm than good. Make a list of your daily, weekly, and monthly tasks and responsibilities.

Also, make a list of ways you speed up your life, such as eating fast food or driving where you can walk. What can you change? In what ways can you slow down and live your daily life more deliberately and with more thoughtful intention? It has not been easy for me, someone who has always maintained a fast-paced and ever-changing lifestyle, but I have come to appreciate a more simplified and structured routine. I feel healthier, happier, and better rested. I save more time and money, and I eat better. My stress levels feel more manageable. Slowing down is an ongoing process; sometimes, it may not be possible financially for you to step away from more fast-paced living. Do an inventory of your habits and get a measurement of your energy expenditure. Then identify your preferred lifestyle and strategize ways to implement it.

While slowing down is obviously about self-care and personal well-being, as is family planning, these lifestyle choices are also about advocating for a sustainable community. The pressure we put on each other to uphold cultural expectations drains the planet as it drains us. We are more than our contributions to economic growth, and in treating ourselves better, we treat others better.

Action, Acceptance, and Hope

"What you do makes a difference, and you have to decide what kind of difference you want to make."—**Dr. Jane Goodall**
(leading naturalist and conservationist)

Humans tend to be drawn to what is convenient, familiar, and predictable. We gravitate to what supports our perspective and fits into our current lifestyle, and we like to assume the best outcome is likely even if we don't change. If a storm is coming, we want to believe it won't be as bad as forecasted. In some ways, it is good that we do this. However, wishful thinking and confirmation bias are not the same as optimism or even hope. Hope does not mean overlooking reality, and acceptance does not mean conceding; both are needed for effective action. To act effectively, we need to accept reality and maintain hope that with work, things can be better. We also need to leave behind the comfort of convenience and familiarity, which gets in the way of progress and necessary change.

I sometimes feel hopeless when I consider the weight of nearly 8 billion people on the planet during this massive crisis of resource management. You, too, may be wondering what difference a person, a family, or even a town can make, pitted against the recklessness of industries and corporations. What can we do to have an impact? We can create safe places to process climate grief together, all the while building climate resilience and devising action steps to mitigate climate change to the extent that we still can. We can create local communities founded upon action, acceptance, and hope so that together, we will be stronger than each of us alone. As cultural anthropologist Margaret Mead said: "Never doubt that a small group of thoughtful, committed citizens can change the world; indeed, it's the only thing that ever has."

The sustainability movement predates the first Earth Day in 1970. There have been people working in their own communities to push back against industrialization, irresponsible resource use, and social and environmental injustices for a long time, probably for as long as these things have existed. As we as a species keep evolving, activists are always on the front lines of progress, pushing us toward better behavior, deeper awareness, and a more inclusive morality. To be hopeful isn't to wait for evidence of potential success before attempting to create change. Rather, it is to believe that our species needs to do better and to set out to prove that we can.

You are not alone in hoping for a brighter future and doing your part by tempering your desire for heating or air conditioning, opting to bike instead of driving, or gardening more. You are not the only one hearing experts talk about climate change and feeling enraged. It is not just you who is inspired by people like Sylvia Earle.[5] The truth is that there are so many people around the world trying to make it a better place. For every Sylvia Earle, there are countless folks just like her, who are often doing things that are just as incredible but who haven't been in the spotlight. Still, they are there, dedicating their entire lives to creating amazing change in their communities. Activists are simply people who are compelled to do something they think needs to be done instead of assuming somebody else will do it. For many of us, the daily barrage of news filled with injustice and instability has been enough to propel us into activism. If you've been preoccupied with your job, relationships, or kids, with saving money, helping family, or focusing on your own health, you can still find ways to participate. It is easier to incorporate activism into your life and make an impact than you may think. Action, acceptance, and hope together will help you thrive and become a powerful influencer in the fight for our climate.

Finding Role Models

"Surround yourself with the risk takers, storytellers, creators, truth seekers, artists, adventures, and dream makers, but mostly surround yourself with the people who draw that same magic out of you."—**Brooke Hampton** (author)

Influencers are those who push new cultural trends and can communicate their own hopes for the future effectively. Rachel Carson was a scientist who inspired a whole new wave of environmental activists with her emotionally charged book about the destruction of a local ecosystem. Jane Goodall is a leading naturalist and conservationist who revolutionized how we understand and relate to other animals and continues to advocate for the environment and nonhuman species. Vandana Shiva is a physicist and food sovereignty activist who has solved many of modern agriculture's problems, all while (like the other two) having to advocate for herself as a woman in science. (Imagine how much more women will get done when equal pay and opportunities don't have to be fought for.) These three women are highly influential. Influence also works on smaller scales. There are influencers encouraging sustainability at the local level, all of whom help move the dial in our favor. Most influencers are not well known; still, their impact extends beyond their own actions. Think of your role models, people in your life who have influenced you to think and act the way you do. Having influence on others multiplies your individual impact by orders of magnitude. It makes your contribution, no matter how small to begin with, incalculable and important.

During my trek across northern Minnesota, I was lucky to be able to interview many local leaders who were fighting valiantly against the mining industry. Everybody I met was a powerful role model and proof that people with typical lifestyles, without superpowers, political power, or endless monetary resources can indeed be powerful changemakers.

Among them, one person who has always stood out to me is a man named Hippie Dan, who lives in Duluth, Minnesota. It didn't take me long to come across Dan. From the Chester Creek Trail near his home to the employee-owned bakery in the neighborhood (from which he is now retired), Hippie Dan leaves a trail of smiles and newly learned knowledge behind him wherever he goes—usually with his two yellow Labs in tow. He's typically wearing tie-dye, hiking boots, an old baseball cap, and his hair in short little pigtails. He knows everybody, and nobody forgets it if they've met him. I first met Hippie Dan on the trail and would cross paths with him nearly every time I went for a run. I had a dog with me and our quick hellos usually included a quip about the dogs, and it was not long before we were chatting more and getting deep into life, philosophy, and sustainability.

Dan has a landline, but good luck catching him at home. He doesn't have a car or a cell phone, and he lives as detached from the power grid as the city will allow. Sustainability and simplicity are what he puts his energy into achieving. He gives to the community daily by maintaining the trail and teaching others about ethical land management. He knows the city's ecosystem better than most. When I interviewed him during my journey— along the small Chester Creek section of the 310-mile trail that I was jogging—he got emotional about the state of the planet. He told me that the grief caused by climate change never leaves him. In fact, it's that grief that seems to motivate him so much to pursue the lifestyle he does. He doesn't just engage in activism. He lives his life in every way in congruence with his values of living simply and keeping his carbon footprint light. He explained that living in the moment, noticing the seasons change, socializing with neighbors, and maintaining a simple rhythm in his daily life all help keep the grief at bay. But it's always there, brought on by the memory of a healthier planet, the loss of indigenous peoples, wisdom, and land, and the destruction of countless special places. Dan reminded me that the best we can do is hold contentment and sadness together, and defend what we know is right through consistent action.

Hippie Dan was one of several people I learned from on the trail who would transform my thinking. From everybody, I learned to build my sense of hope not from looking for evidence to feel hopeful, but from hoping—seeing "hope" as a verb. Before that, I had spent my last day before the run in a research boat on a lake with Dr. Lorena Rios Mendoza, a highly influential chemist and chemistry professor who awoke the nation to the problem of microplastics in our water. I learned from her that good work done in whatever corner of the world will always catalyze good work in other places. From Dr. John Pastor, biology professor, I learned the art of acknowledging painful realities and mourning, all while working to change the outcome. It was a conversation with him that helped me start to understand my own climate grief. I learned how to fight against political pressure from early Sierra Club leaders and their hilarious tale of ingenuity, creativity, and dumb luck, in which they saved a sacred river from being turned into a mine tailings pond and instead had it preserved as part of a state park.

I also learned important traditions around giving, sharing, and showing thanks from Ojibwe tribe members, the original stewards of the northern Minnesota region. Their work against nonrenewable-resource industries is ongoing, as they lead activists through fight after fight to save the land from pipelines and mines. I feel particularly lucky to have been able to connect with Winona LaDuke, indigenous rights advocate and the first Green Party member to receive an electoral vote. She pointed out the need for activists in Minnesota and elsewhere, as well as the insolence of the United States government in arresting clean-water activists, thus: "Someone needs to explain to me why wanting clean drinking water makes you an activist, and why proposing to destroy water with chemical warfare doesn't make a corporation a terrorist."

The geographical area I covered was small, the journey I took relatively short, and the people I encountered mostly unknown to the world. But to the health and well-being of our planet, the work that each of these people does to preserve Lake Superior is immeasurably important. Theirs is one of the countless communities around the world that are pushing for the same justice.

Good Enough

"You've got to get people to believe that change is possible. . . . You have to show that you can fight things successfully even if you don't win."—**Winona LaDuke**
(indigenous rights advocate)

During my run across northern Minnesota, I felt within me an urgent sense that what I was doing wasn't enough. What's more is that the people I was interviewing, despite their amazing accomplishments, told me that they were plagued by a similar urgency, fear, and guilt. Likewise, my clients and friends often say that they don't think they can do enough, or that they look at what others are doing and don't think they can measure up. This is a common misconception of our own value and capacity to create change.

As somebody who has worked in nonprofits my entire career, I can tell you that any and all contributions to the overall mission are priceless. There is no such thing as a volunteer who doesn't give enough! Every little bit helps. When I coach people to create more sustainable yards, I can see the difference one tiny pollinator garden makes in the overall ecosystem of the neighborhood. And as a climate change expert studying *culture* change, I can tell you that when one person does something new, such as adding solar panels to their roof or picking up a weekly volunteer gig, a ripple effect is seen in how their social circle responds. We are social creatures with an innate desire to do good and improve our well-being, and hence mechanisms in our brains that compel us to copy those around us who seem to be doing just that. So, if you ever feel ineffective, reframe your perspective. You may find that even small actions and habits of yours have inspired others to join in.

Keep in mind that statistically, the actions of individuals have a much smaller impact than do those of powerful corporations, industries, and governments. As long as big corporations' destructive behaviors continue to dwarf our personal contributions and sacrifices, the math simply does not add up in the planet's favor. The hardest part about climate grief is accepting that we do not have much control over the outcome. All we can do is make changes in our own lives, all the while continuing to strategize ways to force change from the bigger contributors to the climate crisis. If you don't feel good enough, consider whether you are taking on undue guilt. Once you have done your part, accept that the rest is out of your control. Focus on your own progress rather than berate yourself for what you alone cannot fix.

What If We Were Wrong?

"What if you fail?" A friend asked me this as I was starting on this book.

At that moment, I didn't know what to think or say. I looked at him blankly. "Fail what?"

"Fail at saving the planet," he replied. "What if you put all this work into saving the planet, and it doesn't work? If somebody told you that the world we know would be gone in fifty years, that oceans would be depleted of life, and that we simply would not have managed to curb any of the worst-case scenarios, would you live your life differently right now?"

His question offended me at first, and then I realized this was a question we *all* might have. Our fear of failure is a barrier to fighting climate change.

While this climate crisis is undeniably a human responsibility, nature itself is morally indifferent. Even if we removed all human-caused dangers, injuries, trauma, diseases, and deaths, living in the wild would still be no easy task. In nature, someone with an injured paw or hoof would quickly become a meal for somebody else—somebody else who, without that meal, would starve. Given that wild-animal suffering has always been around, why should we care? If humans are just one more morally flawed or even indifferent species on a planet full of self-serving creatures all living in survival mode, who cares if our actions are now destroying the planet? What if we are wrong to care so much?

To contemplate the suffering that is a de facto part of life on this planet can indeed be demoralizing; personally, I know that I do not like to suffer. I don't like to feel pain or fear, nor do I want any of my actions to cause those feelings in anybody else, human or otherwise. And this is exactly why we urgently need to do what we can to prevent environmental disaster. Widespread pollution, ravaging wildfires stemming from climate change, and other harms to the ecosystem caused by humans only add to the pain that already exists in nature, not to mention to human suffering too. That pain is inevitable in life is no excuse for us not to do what we can to prevent it. So I am working to change my own behaviors that might cause another being fear, pain, or otherwise suffering. Whether, in the end, we succeed in stopping climate change altogether, or eradicating suffering for other animals and ourselves, we can't be sure. But this much I know: the same actions that will ease my own climate grief in the years ahead will also lighten the burdens of those around me. To find meaning in reducing suffering is the best I can do.

Still, with all the uncertainty surrounding us, it becomes easy to doubt ourselves, and when we make mistakes, it is easy to give in to the status quo. It can also feel overwhelming to realize, with every step we take, that there is always more to be done. Trust that as you move along, you will continue to learn and do better. You will learn to accept that progress doesn't have to equal perfection. Each step forward is just that, and it is worthy (even if you feel like you're moving backwards or sideways!). You will realize that you aren't alone in your goals, and you will feel more and more confident with practice. You will create believers among your friends. You will learn when to pull back and take a break, how to care for yourself, and how to rely on others when you're grieving. You will learn how to communicate more effectively and how to manage your fears and feelings. You will learn so much, and there will never be an end to what you can try or the changes you'll encourage. We are all in this together.

The same friend who asked me about failure asked me how I would feel if, decades from now, humankind hadn't changed but the world was still much the same: "What if we never had to panic? What if the planet was doing just fine then?" This was another question that was difficult for me to comprehend at first, as to me, climate change is in so many ways a matter of fact. After some thought, I decided that even if we were wrong, even if climate change were beyond our control or not so bad after all, everything we could be doing to save resources, to expand our compassion, to be kinder and gentler to each other and the planet would still be good and necessary.

Hospice Care for a Dying World

"The saddest day has gleams of light, The darkest wave hath
bright foam beneath it. There twinkles o'er the cloudiest
night, Some solitary star to cheer it."—**Sarah Winnemucca**
(Northern Paiute author, activist, and educator)

If we do indeed find that we are too late, that life as we know
it will change drastically, how do we show up for the planet
and for each other? We will face—indeed, many of us already
have faced—incredible losses. Mining companies will win land
leases; state legislatures will strike down mass transit plans; urban
sprawl will continue as long as our population keeps increasing.
In hospice care, when a patient begins the hospice journey, it
means there will be no additional medical treatments used in an
attempt to cure their disease. Rather, the goal is for them to enjoy
as much comfort, dignity, and peace as possible while waiting
for their impending passing. But even in times like this, much is
unknown. When it comes to climate change, it is impossible for
us to know if or when we have truly reached some tipping point.
Ahead of us are likely many tipping points to come, after which
certain losses would become unavoidable.

A college friend of mine is a hospice chaplain. Her practice is
witnessing death and the dying, and it shows: she moves through
grief with remarkable grace and vulnerability. When I asked her
how she manages to spend every day surrounded by endings,
sadness, and impermanence, she told me that actually, it is easy.
Death is a part of everything, endings are a constant in life, and at
some point, when we realize we don't have control over anything,
that is when everybody can breathe and take in the moment. All
we have to do, then, is exist together in kindness and love.

I do sometimes have days when my grief about climate
change fills me with debilitating sadness. Mostly, though, I go

through days when it feels like someone I love is really ill. When a friend is battling cancer, we do not rescind our friendship. We do not walk away from a fire in our kitchen, assuming it is too late to save the house. We put out the fire and save what we can because we realize that it makes a difference. Some of our efforts are like that. But some of our efforts stem from the acknowledgement that it is simply natural and right to be there, doing the work. When we love something or someone, we stay present.

The Butterfly Effect

According to chaos theory, the butterfly effect is a property of chaotic systems (such as the climate) whereby a miniscule occurrence can lead to much more significant and even unpredictable events in the future. When a butterfly flaps their wings in India, for example, a series of effects is set off that eventually leads to a tornado in Iowa. Chaos theory is a branch of mathematics built on the foundational theory by Edward Lorenz, a meteorology professor. The concept of the butterfly effect also invites a more metaphysical or spiritual perspective. Through any lens, scientific or spiritual, though, this effect represents a powerful unknown.

I have come to believe firmly in the power of small actions by many actors, which accumulate to a big change over time, and I am hopeful that the actions we take now will have powerful implications that we can't yet anticipate. Thinking of ourselves as part of a larger system can produce much hope and motivation, though it may not feel like a realistic perspective. Sometimes I, too, am skeptical of the idea that if more people do just a little bit, we have a chance at changing things. But this is how change has always happened. In any community, a shared workload results in a minimal amount of work for each individual. Successful political campaigns throughout history have often been fueled by many supporters who each gave a small amount. I do believe that when we set an intention and shift our behaviors even just a little, we are contributing to the energy of that intention. You never know. So keep doing the right thing, no matter how small it seems.

What Change Do You Want to Be?

So we took the written words of our philosophers,
And built a fire from it.
Let's get those engines lit.
We took the church's veil and built a mighty sail
To carry forth this ship.
—Cloud Cult's song "There's So Much Energy in Us"

The song quoted above is about being on a long, unfinished journey, finally coming to terms with failure to complete one's mission, but perhaps realizing, in the end, that the mission isn't yet over and that everything one needed to achieve one's goal has been there all along. To me, the imagery of age-old information being used as fuel for starting a fire and a sacred cloth for harnessing the wind reflects a cultural coming of age. When I first heard this song, I thought of climate change and the worldwide mission we are on together. I thought about the many people around the world who are trying to steer our climate in a better direction.

We access so much power within us when we act on our own values, and we inevitably find others already doing the same with whom we can join forces. Suddenly, a whole new world of opportunity opens up. When we decide to do what we think is right, regardless of what those around us seem to be doing, we always come to realize we are not alone. We never were alone. You come to find that there is always somebody just as excited and motivated, just as intuitive, or just as creative as you. There is always somebody already trying to create a new world in their backyard—the same world you want to see.

Revolutions are brought about by individuals who believe in the impossible and join together to demand that the impossible become reality. If we all make the same commitment to improving the world like our lives depend on it, we will be surprised by the power we truly possess.

Maybe you've already seen this hold true in your own life. Think about what you were doing ten years ago. Did you imagine you would be where you are today? What major obstacles were you facing ten years ago that you could not imagine overcoming? Maybe you were going through a divorce and have since found a new and better life being on your own. Or perhaps you moved to a new city and had no idea how much that would shape your life in a positive way. Did you graduate? Start a business? Change your political affiliation? Build your confidence? You are proof that change is not only possible but inevitable. While it may seem idealistic, woo-woo, or overly simplistic to say we can manifest the future, human history proves it to be true. Your next step is to decide what role you want to take on. Be open to grief, maybe even failure, but do not give in to them, and you will keep open the precious doors of uncertainty and potential. Do what you need to do to live your own best life. Work hard, take responsibility, and rest when you need to. Forgive yourself, love yourself, and give the same grace to everybody you know. Just don't do nothing. The world will change if and when you do.

AFTERWORD

Aubrey H. Fine

Professor Emeritus California Polytechnic State University, Pomona; and author

When Dr. Weaver asked me to write the foreword for her book, I initially was puzzled about her request. I was truly honored; however, I questioned my credentials and my expertise in the area. For sure, I'm an advocate for human-animal interactions and appreciate the significance of these encounters. As a boy, growing up in Canada, I never had animals in my life, but as a young adult, I quickly learned to appreciate their significance and involvement in our daily lives. Now after so many decades I contend animals enhance and enrich in countless ways our souls and lifestyles. These human-animal interactions profoundly deepen our appreciation of our world. The more I thought about Dr. Weaver's invitation, the more I realized that I had insights that could add to her argument.

The world is changing and is very different from previous centuries. A few years back, I went up to Churchill Manitoba to visit the wildlife. While visiting, I observed firsthand how the environment in the north was changing and how complicated it was for polar bears to survive. The snowcapped spaces were much more limited, and consequently the polar bears had a harder time in their daily survival.

I am reminded of a quotation by Jacques-Yves Cousteau who stated that "Centuries ago man had to fight nature to survive. In this century, man is beginning to realize that, to survive, he must protect it." Although written simply, it succinctly shares a message that must be embraced. We are the guardians of this world, and without proper care or because of selfish disregard, we could lose our most important treasure.

It's ironic that Dr. Weaver's presentation of climate grief applied Kübler-Ross's stages of loss to explain what and how some humans are experiencing when mourning the world that they are possibly losing. One thing I realized quickly was, although we are grieving the changes that are occurring in climate today, we still have an opportunity to become the change that is needed. It is incumbent on our civilization to do what it must to preserve our globe for future generations to enjoy and appreciate. We are the gatekeepers for the future and must preserve the environment so that future generations will flourish. Our selfishness, in prioritizing our comfort for today, is having a dramatic impact on future generations' ability to relish what exists right now.

The world population today is growing incrementally, and the globe is shrinking rather than expanding. Climate change only makes this equation even more complicated when we pollute the waters and the land that we most importantly need. Al Gore, in his book *An Inconvenient Truth*, wanted to illustrate some of the realities we face if we don't change our ways. The key words are changing our ways so that we can preserve our world for tomorrow. Al Gore gave voice to the recognition that we are all responsible for the preservation of this world and are likewise responsible for the consequent global results of our unmended actions. It may be easy to ignore what is occurring, but much more challenging to truly make a difference. Margaret Mead once thoughtfully said, "A small group of thoughtful people could change the world. Indeed, it's the only thing that ever has." The leadership do not need to be politicians or celebrities, but normal citizens who want to make a difference. For example, in 2018 Greta Thunberg started school strikes in Sweden to bring attention to the importance of making a difference in climate change. There are some who jeered her efforts, but eventually Greta became internationally known as an ambassador for making a difference. Her efforts have made an impact in getting governments to begin making a change in carbon emissions and to follow the Paris agreement.

When we grieve loss, we do go through many stages, including denial, bargaining, and anger. At some point for those who successfully navigate through the process of mourning, they get to the stage of acceptance. I argue that it is incumbent upon all of us not to get to that stage of acceptance and deny that climate change is real and cannot be changed. We need to put into action a plan for change and enjoy what we have before it is forever lost.

Dr. Weaver's presentation not only gives a good overview of the changes that are occurring globally regarding climate and the emissions, but also gives strong information about what we need to do to enjoy the environment we live in. The theory of biophilia by E. O. Wilson truly helps us understand that we humans have an innate predisposition to enjoy the world we live in. I appreciated the content within Weaver's text, especially Chapter 4, where she provides some solutions suggesting where we go from here. It is crucial for all of us to make decisions on sustainability and the importance of our interactions with the environment and the living world. Her description of nature-based therapeutic services and the whole field of Ecopsychology was quite revealing. She defines Ecopsychology as the field that is centered around how humans interact with nature. The theory of biophilia describes how humans have this innate predisposition with the living environment. Steven Kellert, in his book *Birthright: People and Nature in the Modern World*, stated we will never be truly healthy, satisfied, or fulfilled if we live apart and alienated from the environment from which we evolved. These words resonate very accurately the sentiment of one of the messages within this book. We must appreciate the importance of making a connection to our living world, and our commitment to take care of it. Weaver provides attention to the 3Rs as they pertain to sustainability in our environment. The slogan "reduce, reuse, recycle" was initially established in in the 1970s, but its meaning is still appropriate as we battle climate change today.

Over the past five decades, I have worked with many individuals in the field of animal assisted therapy, incorporating the tenets of biophilia into my therapeutic regime. I have personally witnessed not only the healing benefits of interacting with companion animals and therapy animals, but the therapeutic value of people enjoying and engaging in the environment they live in. Gardening and hiking have been considered as healthy outlets that people benefit from therapeutically. It's now common that when people feel tired or overstimulated, they turn to nature as an outlet for enrichment. This type of approach was discussed quite well in Weaver's subsection on holistically sustainable lifestyles.

As I end this short essay, I'm reminded of the Native American proverb that elegantly states that we don't inherit the Earth from our ancestors, we borrow it for our children. We must take these words very seriously as we address the significance of climate change. Perhaps then we can somewhat assuage our grief for having so thoughtlessly and recklessly allowed the desecration of our world. It is incumbent upon all of us to seriously consider the consequences of our misjudgments and make choices to better the world not only for today but for tomorrow.

We have often been warned by numerous world leaders to heed our actions. Kofi Annan, former UN Secretary-General, summarizes what is on the minds of many with regards to this dilemma. He emphasizes that the world is reaching the tipping point beyond which climate change may become irreversible. He ends his argument by articulating, "If this happens, we risk denying present and future generations the right to a healthy and sustainable planet—the whole of humanity stands to lose." Reading this book may not stop this horrific problem but will provide you with some insights on your role in sustaining and cherishing the world we live in today.

ENDNOTES

Chapter 1

1. It is thought that the Mayan civilization fell after overpopulation, combined with significant drought, led to violent competition for resources. More than 4,000 years ago, the Akkadian Empire of Mesopotamia fell to a 300-year drought that, even with frequent migration, they could not escape. In the past, many communities facing severe climate change and ecosystem collapse tended to migrate. That is not an option in the current climate emergency.

2. Theodore Roszak is credited for coining the term "ecopsychology" in his 1992 book *The Voice of the Earth*. He describes ecopsychology as a tool for bridging the gulf between the psychological and the ecological, as well as for seeing humanity's needs on a continuum with the needs of the planet.

3. While most of us have been culturally conditioned to accept heavy meat consumption as the norm, there is ample evidence that our bodies thrive best on the vitamins and minerals consumed from a variety of plants. *How Not to Die: Discover the Foods Scientifically Proven to Prevent and Reverse Disease* by Michael Greger is one of the most well-known resources on the science behind a whole-foods, plant-based diet. There are many other resources by a variety of nutritionists, doctors, athletic trainers, and more.

4. Seasonal Affective Disorder is a diagnosable mood disorder that occurs most often in winter climates. Anecdotes from my clients suggest they often struggle through the winter months.

5. Despite our separation from nature, we still have many nature-based practices such as daylight saving time and religious rituals tied to moon cycles (Easter, Christmas, the Buddhist festival of Vesak, and the Muslim celebration of Ramadan, to name just a few).

6. There are over 4,000 species of bees in the United States alone, and they are needed to pollinate many foods humans consume. About one-third of our food grows on plants pollinated by honeybees. Bees are considered keystone species in many regions, meaning that with bees extinct, we would see ecosystem collapse.

7. Lack of clean water is one of the worst global problems. Unsanitary conditions (no water treatment system in densely populated areas, no hand washing available, and so on) allow otherwise avoidable pathogens to take hold and threaten entire communities. Because humans have a long digestive tract that gives viruses and bacteria ample time to be absorbed, we are susceptible to these pathogens.

8. While we are susceptible to being harmed by bad bacteria, we need good bacteria and other healthy microbes, which we consume with our food. To grow fruits and vegetables, we need "healthy" topsoil that has an abundance and variety of minerals and microbes. There are more microbes in a tiny spoonful of soil than there are people on Earth.

9. Known as indoor vertical farming, this practice enables us to produce larger amounts of food with a smaller footprint. It requires less space, fewer resources, and no pesticides or herbicides. While there are disadvantages, indoor vertical farming is one innovation with the potential to help us sustain life on the planet.

10. Cell-based meat and dairy products grown from cell cultures have challenged our understanding of proteins and of life itself. Plant-based "meat" and "dairy" are created from only non-animal sources, generally requiring less water and land and causing minimal animal suffering.

11. While we have long used energy from the sun for passive solar heat, technological advances are quickly enabling the use of solar power at industrial levels. Current solar-power technologies have their downsides, but investments in this field could yield sustainable and far less damaging variations in the near future.

12. The Neolithic Period spanned from 10,000 BCE to 4,500 BCE and marked the domestication of some animal species, the beginning of agricultural and animal-exploiting practices we still heavily rely on to this day.

13. To thoroughly understand the human autonomic nervous system requires a deep dive into a neuropsychology textbook, but simply put, you can feel this system kick in anytime a stressor makes your heart rate jump and your energy increase. The sudden burst of hyper-alertness and anxiety is indicative of this system working to help you quickly respond to said stressor.

14. "Burnout" is a buzzword that puts the onus on the individual to deal with the problem rather than on the cultural pressures that lead to it in the first place. As it is used, however, the term encompasses a group of symptoms frequently described by activists.

15. Mahzarin R. Banaji and Anthony G. Greenwald's *Blindspot: Hidden Biases of Good People* is a great book that explores our brains' deeply embedded prejudices carried over from our species' early survival strategies. The book outlines how groupthink is driven by our willingness to conform even to unethical behavior, and how racism is lurking in the subconscious of even the most progressive people.

16. *Green Fire*, a documentary about Aldo Leopold's life and career, describes how he came to realize he needed to develop a more just and holistic conservation ethic.

17. Systems thinking, which will be addressed in the coming chapters, is a strategy for understanding the world as a system of relationships, as an interconnected whole. Compared to a linear view of the world or an interpretation of it as its parts, this helps us better grasp the complexities of our reality, as well as the perspectives of other people and other beings.

18. Obesity, heart disease, depression and anxiety, drug and alcohol problems, and suicide are just some of the ailments that have been on a steady increase in the post-WWII era. This is likely due to several lifestyle factors, including decreased physical activity and time spent outside, shifting cultural pressures, compromised food and water safety, and more recently, increased use of personal electronic devices.

19. Comparisons of incomes and giving in the United States show a consistent trend that poorer populations are the most charitable demographic, giving a higher percentage of their incomes than do wealthy people.

20. The National Oceanic and Atmospheric Administration (NOAA), the Environmental Protection Agency (EPA), the Woods Hole Oceanographic Institution (WHOI), and the European Environment Agency (EEA) are the sources used for collecting the most current scientific measurements and for estimating factors of climate change, including ocean acidification.

21. AI is the abbreviation for artificial intelligence, which, at the time of this writing, is already smarter than humans in many instances.

22. My favorite resources for learning more about capitalism and how it is enmeshed with climate change and injustice include any book by Naomi Klein, John Sorenson's *Constructing Ecoterrorism*, Will Potter's *Green Is the New Red*, and Edward Abbey's *The Monkey Wrench Gang*.

Chapter 2

1. A fuller description of denial is available on page 8 of Elisabeth Kübler-Ross and David Kessler's book *On Grief and Grieving*; on subsequent pages, anger, bargaining, sadness, and acceptance are also fully explained.

2. Billy Joel's "Piano Man" is one of the many songs about using escapism to cope with grief. Clearly, this resonates with the masses, as the song is a crowd favorite.

3. Check out Michael Specter's book *Denialism: How Irrational Thinking Hinders Scientific Progress, Harms the Planet, and Threatens Our Lives*.

4. This comparison appears in the aforementioned book *On Grief and Grieving*. Another one of Elisabeth Kübler-Ross's books, *On Death and Dying*, is also a good resource for learning about grief, though it is focused more on the first-person experience of facing one's own impending death.

5. David Kessler's book on the topic is *Finding Meaning, the Sixth Stage of Grief*.

Chapter 3

1. More information about the study, completed in 2017, can be found on adultdevelopmentstudy.org. Harvard's research on healthy aging is ongoing.

2. Being wholehearted is defined as having a sincere devotion to or unreserved enthusiasm about something. Brown describes her research on wholehearted living in multiple TED Talks, books, and other writings.

3. Minnesota Nice is a stereotype of the region's culture that implies people here are mild-mannered, reserved, accommodating, neighborly, and loyal. On a darker side, the stereotype is that in an attempt to avoid direct conflict, people tend to be passive-aggressive and gossipy and to keep newcomers at a distance.

Chapter 4

1. From the 1992 anthology *Ecopsychology: Restoring the Earth, Healing the Mind*.

2. Drs. Will Allen and Margaret Kilvington define systems thinking as the practice of "examining the linkages and interactions between the elements that comprise the whole of a system."

3. One book on the topic is *Systems Thinking for Social Change: A Practical Guide to Solving Complex Problems, Avoiding Unintended Consequences, and Achieving Lasting Results* by David Peter Stroh.

4. This was discussed in several sources, including *Time* magazine, in December 2020.

5. Sylvia Earle is an American marine biologist who served as the NOAA's first female chief scientist, who educates about the havoc wreaked by the commercial fishing industry and encourages plant-based eating. She was featured in the 2021 documentary *Seaspiracy*.

BIBLIOGRAPHY

Abbey, Edward. *The Monkey Wrench Gang*. Salt Lake City: Dream Garden Press, 1985.

Allen, Will, and Margaret Kilvington. "Learning and working together for the environment: applying the Integrated Systems for Knowledge Management approach." *Development Bulletin*, no. 58 (July 2002), pp. 106–110.

"Ancient Civilizations: The Secrets of Lost Empires." *History Channel*. November 22, 2019.

Banaji, Mahzarin R., and Anthony G. Greenwalk. *Blindspot: Hidden Biases of Good People*. New York: Delacorte Press, 2013.

Brown, Brené. *Atlas of the Heart: Mapping Meaningful Connection and the Language of Human Experience*. New York: Random House, 2021.

Canty, J. M. (ed.). *Ecological and Social Healing: Multicultural Women's Voices*. New York: Routledge, 2017.

Capra, Fritjof. *The Hidden Connections: Integrating the Biological, Cognitive, and Social Dimensions of Life into a Science of Sustainability*. New York: Random House, 2002.

Carson, Rachel. *Silent Spring*. Boston: Houghton Mifflin, 1962.

Coyote, Peter, et al. *Green Fire: Aldo Leopold and a Land Ethic for Our Time*. Baraboo, Wisconsin: Aldo Leopold Foundation, 2011.

Dholakia, Utpal. "Why People Who Have Less Give More." *Psychology Today*. November 20, 2017. https://www.psychologytoday.com/us/blog/the-science-behind-behavior/201711/why-people-who-have-less-give-more.

Edwards, Andres R. *Thriving beyond Sustainability: Pathways to a Resilient Society*. Gabriola Island, Canada: New Society Publishers, 2010.

Greger, Michael, and Gene Stone. *How Not to Die: Discover the Foods Scientifically Proven to Prevent and Reverse Disease*. London: Macmillan, 2016.

Johnson, A. E., and K. K. Wilkinson (eds.). *All We Can Cave: Truth, Courage, and Solutions for the Climate Crisis.* New York: Penguin Random House, 2020.

Harding, Stephan. *Animate Earth: Science, Intuition, and Gaia.* White River Junction, Vermont: Chelsea Green Publishing, 2006.

Harvard Medical School. *Adult Development Study.* 2015. https://www.adultdevelopmentstudy.org/.

Kessler, David. *Finding Meaning: The Sixth Stage of Grief.* New York: Scribner, 2019.

Kjellgren, Eric, and Jennifer Wagelie. "Easter Island." *Heilbrunn Timeline of Art History.* New York: The Metropolitan Museum of Art, 2000–. http://www.metmuseum.org/toah/hd/eais/hd_eais.htm (October 2002).

Klein, Naomi. *This Changes Everything: Capitalism vs. the Climate.* New York: Simon & Schuster, 2015.

Kolbert, Elizabeth. *The Sixth Extinction: An Unnatural History.* New York: Picador, 2014.

Kübler-Ross, Elisabeth. *On Death and Dying: What the Dying Have to Teach Doctors, Nurses, Clergy, and Their Own Families.* New York: Scribner, 1993.

Kübler-Ross, Elisabeth, and David Kessler. *On Grief and Grieving: Finding the Meaning of Grief through the Five Stages of Loss.* New York: Scribner, 2005.

Leenaert, Tobias. *How to Create a Vegan World: A Pragmatic Approach.* New York: Lantern Books, 2017.

Macy, Joanna, and Chris Johnstone. *Active Hope: How to Face the Mess We're in without Going Crazy.* Navato, CA: New World Library, 2012.

Michener, Charles D. *The Bees of the World.* Baltimore: Johns Hopkins University Press, 2002.

Montrie, Chad. *The Myth of Silent Spring: Rethinking the Origins of American Environmentalism.* Oakland: University of California Press, 2018.

Partonen, T., and S. R. Pandi-Perumal (eds.). *Seasonal Affective Disorder: Practice and Research.* New York: Oxford University Press, 2010.

Pastor, John. *What Should a Clever Moose Eat? Natural History, Ecology, and the North Woods.* Washington, DC: Island Press, 2016.

Pipher, Mary. *The Green Boat: Reviving Ourselves in Our Capsized Culture.* New York: Riverhead Books, 2013.

Pollan, Michael. *In Defense of Food: An Eater's Manifesto*. New York: Penguin Books, 2008.

Potter, Will. *Green Is the New Red: An Insider's Account of a Social Movement under Siege*. San Francisco: City Light Publishers, 2011.

Purdy, Chase. *Billion Dollar Burger: Inside Big Tech's Race for the Future of Food*. New York: Penguin Random House, 2020.

Roszak, Theordore, et al. *Ecopsychology: Restoring the Earth, Healing the Mind*. Chattanooga: Centerpoint Press, 1995.

Roszak, Theodore. *The Voice of the Earth: An Exploration of Ecopsychology*. Boston: Phanes Press, 1992.

Shiva, Vandana. *Earth Democracy: Justice, Sustainability, and Peace*. Cambridge, Massachussetts: South End Press, 2005.

Solnit, Rebecca. *A Paradise Built in Hell: The Extraordinary Communities that Arise in Disaster*. New York: Penguin Books, 2009.

Sorenson, John. *Constructing Ecoterrorism: Capitalism, Speciesism, and Animal Rights*. Black Point, Nova Scotia, Canada: Fernwood Publishing, 2016.

Specter, Michael. *Denialism: How Irrational Thinking Hinders Scientific Progress, Harms the Planet, and Threatens Our Lives*. New York: Penguin Press, 2009.

Stephens, Anne. *Ecofeminism and Systems Thinking*. London: Routledge, 2013.

Stroh, David Peter. *Systems Thinking for Social Change: A Practical Guide to Solving Complex Problems, Avoiding Unintended Consequences, and Achieving Lasting Results*. White River Junction, Vermont: Chelsea Green Publishing, 2015.

Walters, Sam. "Seven Groundbreaking Ancient Civilizations that Inform Us Today." *Discover*. December 1, 2021. https://www.discovermagazine.com/planet-earth/7-groundbreaking-ancient-civilizations-that-influence-us-today.

Weaver, Shawna. *Nature-Based Therapeutic Service: Sustainability through Individual Holistic Wellness*. Ann Arbor: Proquest, 2015.

Weil, Zoe. *Most Good, Least Harm: A Simple Principle for a Better World and Meaningful Life*. New York: Simon & Schuster, 2009.

ABOUT THE AUTHOR

 **SHAWNA WEAVER** is a career-long educator and mental health advocate. She spent her early career as a mental health therapist and school counselor. The climate crisis compelled her to return to graduate school to earn a PhD in Sustainability Education and explore the intersection of nature and human wellness. She has presented on environmental justice topics to audiences all over North America, Australia, and Europe. She is currently focused on education program development, household sustainability, and wellness advocacy. When she isn't working or traveling, she is home in northern Minnesota, exploring trails with her three-legged canine companion.

ABOUT THE PUBLISHER

LANTERN PUBLISHING & MEDIA was was founded in 2020 to follow and expand on the legacy of Lantern Books—a publishing company started in 1999 on the principles of living with a greater depth and commitment to the preservation of the natural world. Like its predecessor, Lantern Publishing & Media produces books on animal advocacy, veganism, religion, social justice, humane education, psychology, family therapy, and recovery. Lantern is dedicated to printing in the United States on recycled paper and saving resources in our day-to-day operations. Our titles are also available as ebooks and audiobooks.

To catch up on Lantern's publishing program,
visit us at www.lanternpm.org.

facebook.com/lanternpm
twitter.com/lanternpm
instagram.com/lanternpm